THE AUTHENTIC
Tudor & Stuart
DOLLS' HOUSE

BRIAN LONG

GUILD OF MASTER CRAFTSMAN PUBLICATIONS LTD

First published 2006 by
Guild of Master Craftsman Publications Ltd
Castle Place, 166 High Street
Lewes, East Sussex BN7 1XU

Text © Brian Long 2006
© in the work GMC Publications Ltd

ISBN 1 86108 406 4

A catalogue record for this book is available from the
British Library.

Production Manager: Hilary MacCallum
Managing Editor: Gerrie Purcell
Project Editor: Gill Parris
Art Adviser: Andy Humm

Cover and book designer: Ian Hunt Design
Colour reproduction by Wyndeham Graphics
Printed in China by Hing Yip Printing Co., Ltd.

ACKNOWLEDGEMENTS

All black and white line drawings by Brian Long, with
the exception of:

Page 45: Drawings taken from the Antique Collectors' Club
edition of *A History of English Brickwork* by Nathaniel
Lloyd, published in 1983, Woodbridge, Suffolk

Photographs of models by Anthony Bailey. All other
photographs by Brian Long, except where otherwise
stated:

Page 79: Palace of Huntly, reproduced courtesy of
RCAHMS and The National Trust for Scotland

Pages 164–5: Ceiling at Crathes Castle, reproduced
courtesy of The National Trust for Scotland Photo Library

CREDITS

Page 2: Game and hams made by Bob Vincent, of
Country Contrasts

Page 15 and front cover: Late Tudor dolls' house made
by Vic Newey of Redditch

Page 37: 1/12 scale cottage with thatched roof made by
Graham John Wood, of Little Homes of England

Pages 98 (top left) and 100: Model clockwork spit jack
made by G. Lewis, Small Scale

Page 111 (top right): Dishes of food made by Merry
Gourmet Miniatures

Page 182 (bottom right): Section of a model dovecote,
made by Ruth B. King of King Dovecotes

PLEASE NOTE:

All locations are in England,
unless otherwise stated.

CONTENTS

HISTORICAL REFERENCE

The Tudors and Stuarts (originally from the House of Stewart) were related, but ruled over nations that did not agree on many issues. The Tudors claimed sovereignty over parts of France, and were at war with the French. The Stuarts, on the other hand, were related to the French royal family and were their closest ally. Typical of the politics of the period, when Elizabeth I – the last of the Tudors – died without issue, James VI, King of Scotland, inherited the throne and styled himself King of France. From that time on, he changed the spelling of his name from the Scottish 'Stewart' to the French 'Stuart'.

The Stuart era was long, but broken in the middle by the Commonwealth under Oliver Cromwell. The part of the Stuart tenure of interest to us is 1603-1625, when James ('Jacob' in Latin) reigned, giving us the Jacobean period and allowing the Tudor dolls' house enthusiast some leeway in furnishing, using early but basic upholstery which was found in upper-class homes, along with china imported by the East India Company.

1350 1375 1400 1425 1450 1475 1500 1525 1550 1575 1600 1625 1650 1675 1700 1725 1750 1775
A.D.   A.D.

HOUSE OF STEWART
(ruling dynasty of Scotland)

- 1371–90 Robert II
- 1390–1406 Robert III
- 1406–37 James I
- 1437–60 James II
- 1460–88 James III
- 1488–1513 James IV, married Margaret Tudor
- 1513–42 James V
- 1542–67 Mary, Queen of Scots, married Francis II of France, Lord Darnley and the Earl of Bothwell
- 1567 James VI of Scotland (son of Lord Darnley) Became James I of England in 1603

HOUSE OF TUDOR
(ruling dynasty of England)

- 1485–1509 Henry VII
- 1509–47 Henry VIII
- 1547–53 Edward VI
- 1553–58 Mary I, married Philip II of Spain
- 1558–1603 Elizabeth I

HOUSE OF STUART
(England and Scotland united)

- 1603–1625 James I England and VI of Scotland
- 1625–49 Charles I
- 1649–60 Commonwealth *(Interregnum)*
- 1660–85 Charles II

NOTE ON MEASUREMENTS
The standard dolls' house scales are 1/12 and 1/24, both originally based on imperial measurements: in 1/12 scale, one inch represents one foot. Although many craftspeople now use metric measurements, dolls' house hobbyists in Britain and especially America still use feet and inches. Projects in this book are for the 1/12 scale dolls' house. Imperial measurements are given first, followed by their metric equivalent in brackets. Accuracy to the millimetre is generally inappropriate, and metric measurements may be rounded up or down a little for convenience. Never mix imperial and metric measurements – always use one or the other.

INTRODUCTION

When you decided to build a Tudor or Stuart dolls' house you probably had a firm idea of what it was that you wanted. This definitive sourcebook is packed with authentic details, and will show you how to achieve your ambitions.

In fact the terms 'Tudor' and 'Stuart' are more periods in history than any one particular architectural style. Crowned heads gave their names to architectural periods and styles of furniture, but this was only a rough guide, as people did not drop their tools on the death of a monarch, then pick them up the next day to work in an entirely different way. All styles had their roots in an earlier one – if not the one before that – and took a long time to mature; most never died out completely, but rather fell out of fashion.

Generally, the earliest surviving houses were built by someone from a high position in society, as the houses of the majority of the population were poorly constructed, and had to be rebuilt every generation or so. It wasn't until the late sixteenth century that houses were built in more permanent materials.

▲ **Half-timbered houses come in various hues**
This yellow ochre and bleached-oak house shows that Tudor, when half-timbered, is not just black and white (other examples shown overleaf).

▲ Pink with dark oak, red with bleached oak and yellow with stained oak

▲ Yellow with bleached oak

▲ All white

▲ Pink with bleached oak

The choice of building material has always been limited by what was available locally and this in turn was dictated by geology and climate, rather than the influence – or lack of influence – of any monarch. In the uplands and north of Britain the houses were mainly of stone, turf or unbaked earth, while in the south and east they were of timber-framed construction. All of these houses were Tudor or Jacobean, so there was not one style but rather one period, and Tudor is not just black and white, half-timbered, but can be any material that was to hand.

The population at large had a limited number of pigments available to them to use on the decoration of their houses, inside and out. The colours depended, originally, on the local geology and the minerals available to make the pigments: yellow ochre from Oxfordshire, umber from Devon and Cornwall, and red ochre from Devon are still among the best and most permanent pigments used today.

There are paints on the market now specifically for historic houses and, by mixing colours, you can achieve an authentic colour for your dolls' house.

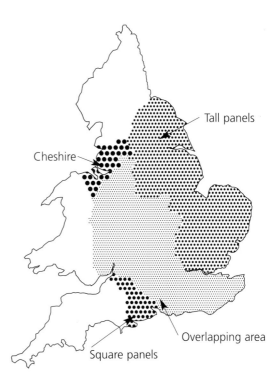

▲ **Diagram showing how timber-frame styles are now distributed in England and the Welsh marshes**
The different panel styles are traditional in some areas and in others they overlap. The most ornate work is in Cheshire.

Timber-framed houses were common in most of England, but found in fewer numbers in Ireland, Scotland and Wales, as well. The cruck frame is perhaps the oldest form, consisting of curved timbers or blades which formed a series of arches to carry not only the roof but to hang the walls onto. Crucks – which are found most in Scotland, northern England down the Pennines and into the Welsh Marches – were also used in many stone-built houses.

Box-framed construction is found mainly in the east and south of England. Box frames were set on a low stone foundation and braces were used to strengthen the corners of the box. A house can consist of several boxes or bays. The many ways used to fill the box using horizontal rails and vertical studs are again regional but, once in place, all that remained to do was fill the gaps between the timbers to keep out the elements.

Close studding, the massing of vertical timbers way beyond what was required to hold the wall up, is found in the west of England, then south of the river Thames, east into Kent, while the delightful use of panel framing is centred on Cheshire and parts of the West Midlands.

▲ **A cruck-frame cottage in Gloucestershire, England**

House in Gilesgate, Hexham, Northumberland, England

The house below (now demolished) may look like a Cotswold-type house, but is in fact typical of stone-building areas in most of England. The angle of pitch in a roof depends largely on the weight of slabs being used and the lighter Cotswold stones have a pitch of anything from 45° to 60°, while the heavier Pennine roofs are not so steep. A period dolls' house chimney does not have to be perfect, as most of the time they were not, as the kitchen one had to be rebuilt again and again and even roofing in the same area had to be re-worked.

So even in areas where it may be safe to say black-and-white half-timbered buildings are Tudor, there are strong regional variations.

Some areas are traditionally built in stone. The type of stone, and the ease with which it could be worked, dictated how ornate or otherwise the stone carving could be. But it was to a large extent fashion that determined the shapes of doors, windows, fireplaces, chimneys and numerous small things, including furniture.

It sounds strange but, if on a journey from north to south you kept an ear open for change of dialect, when you opened your eyes you would see a parallel change of building technique or material. You would start with tower houses for the rich and black houses for the poor, yet by the time you reached the south of England you would find a wealth of timber-framed houses and palaces of brick or stone.

B. Long.

Brick was an important building material, but again only found in certain areas, be they where the raw material, clay, was to be found or where the transport of the period could reach. Then, as now, transporting building materials was expensive, so only the rich used other than local materials. As water was the main form of transport, the best brick houses are by navigable rivers or in clay-producing areas.

Brick came in many colours – mainly variations of red – but white and a dull yellow brick were also made and used in quantity, often being mistaken for stone. Roof tiles could be natural materials, or baked clay and there are marked variations in hue from Scotland down through England.

Mud or unbaked earth was also used. Although we accept this as a building technique in desert regions, we tend to forget there are many houses of this type in the United Kingdom, where this material is referred to as 'cob'. Cob is a mixture of clay and straw, much used in Devon, Dorset and the Solway areas of England and Scotland, with lesser pockets elsewhere.

Cob walls are smooth with rounded corners, and in our climate had to be protected with a 'straw hat' of thatch and shoes of stone. It is not unusual to see the tops of cob walls with the above-mentioned thatch, tile, brick or stone copings to prevent rain penetrating, and a brick or stone plinth to prevent rising damp.

These regional details help give us the many variations we find attractive, but which locals were obliged to use, as it was the very ground they lived and worked on, the local geology that dictated the materials available to them.

Politics was another factor, with the relatively untroubled south having more than its share of comfortable manor houses, while in Ireland, northern England and Scotland, the animosity between nations, clans and non-native settlers meant that the offices normally associated with just such a manor house had to be stacked one on top of another, forming a stout but defensive tower.

While the tower houses of Ireland, Scotland and northern England developed at the same time in history, they did so in three completely different ways and, with a little practice, you can tell the nationality of each house. What they all have in common is the fact that, to gain security in a troubled area, accommodation extended vertically,

▲ **Low Hirst, Ashington, Northumberland, England**
Semi-fortified house with a first-floor entry.

in towers up to 70ft (21m) high, rather than being arranged in a long line, or around a courtyard as in the south of England. If you could not afford a tower then you built a house where the main living area was on the first floor, with the basement being a stout storage area.

Two grand schemes were drawn up, to protect people who were loyal subjects of the crown, which included a border marked by an earthwork and a series of 'strong houses', be they towers or peles (first-floor dwellings), such as Low Hirst, above. One of these earthworks was in Northumberland, and the other was in Ireland, forming a fence around Dublin and giving rise to the saying 'Beyond the Pale', the pale being the earthwork inside which all so-called 'decent' people lived.

So what started out as a search for a house of a particular period has resulted in a choice from an array of styles, materials and techniques, which are all true to period but with distinct regional, even national, variations due to many influences. Which style will you choose for your dolls' house?

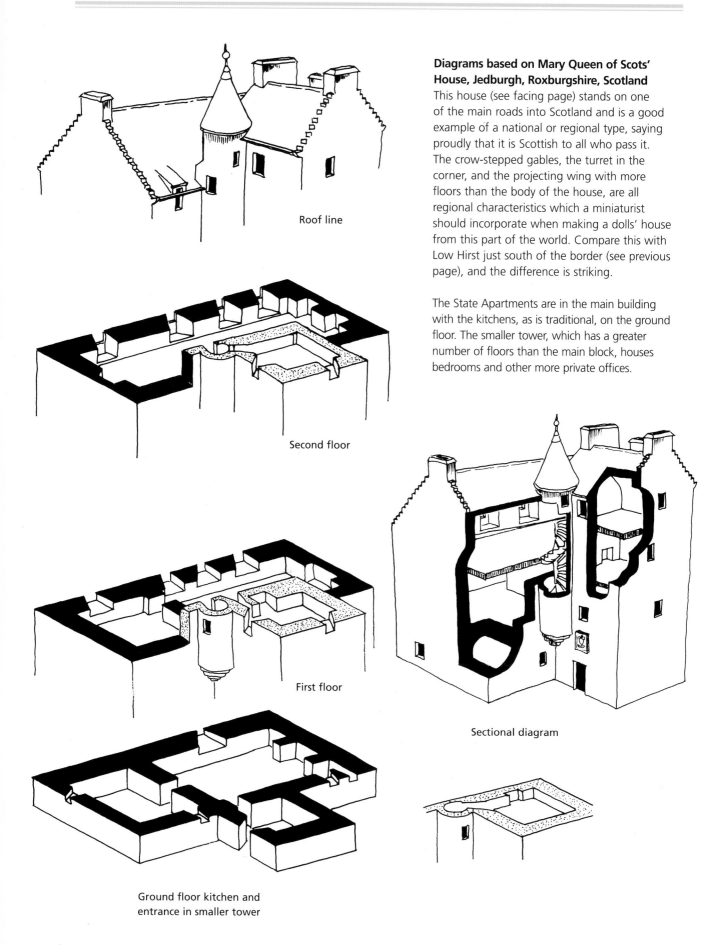

Roof line

Second floor

First floor

Ground floor kitchen and
entrance in smaller tower

**Diagrams based on Mary Queen of Scots'
House, Jedburgh, Roxburghshire, Scotland**
This house (see facing page) stands on one
of the main roads into Scotland and is a good
example of a national or regional type, saying
proudly that it is Scottish to all who pass it.
The crow-stepped gables, the turret in the
corner, and the projecting wing with more
floors than the body of the house, are all
regional characteristics which a miniaturist
should incorporate when making a dolls' house
from this part of the world. Compare this with
Low Hirst just south of the border (see previous
page), and the difference is striking.

The State Apartments are in the main building
with the kitchens, as is traditional, on the ground
floor. The smaller tower, which has a greater
number of floors than the main block, houses
bedrooms and other more private offices.

Sectional diagram

▲ **Traditional Scottish Tower House (16th century)**
Mary Queen of Scots' House, Jedburgh, Scotland

CRAIGIEVAR CASTLE
(1610-1626)

———

The engraving of Craigievar (left), by nineteenth-century engraver R. W. Billings, shows one of Scotland's most distinctive houses, where symmetry was never intended. Its height and broken, confused silhouette give it majesty.

CHAPTER ONE

THE HALF-TIMBERED HOUSE

Timber Frames • Panel-Framed Construction • Adapting a Basic Dolls' House
• Filling the Gap: Wattle and Daub • Covering the Gap: Pargeting • Roofing

TIMBER FRAMES

In this section we will look at timber, the regional variations in the amount used, and the way in which this resulted in wall treatments with a distinctly local character.

Timber-framed houses are often referred to as half-timbered. This does not mean that they are constructed of one part timber and one part some other material, but that the timber used in their framework has been split, riven or halved. Traditional timber frames were usually intended to be exposed to view, but the spaces between had to be filled. Many kinds of infill were used, wattle and daub being the most common one (infills are discussed in 'Filling the Gap', on pages 27–9).

The frames were prefabricated, and the buildings erected on site. Houses built with large-panelled frames appear to have come along first. Examples of these can be found in all areas of Britain where timber-framed construction was used, with numerous types of brace within the panels to make them more rigid. The panels were arranged in decorative groups and filled with either close studding or ornate arrangements of braces forming all sorts of intricate patterns, as well as simple close studding, or close panelling, giving a much smaller and neater arrangement.

Frames with smaller panels are basically large frames with smaller ones, or studding, within them; in Britain these are found predominantly in the west. Instead of a row of panels of room height, each floor had rows of two or three panels to the height of one floor.

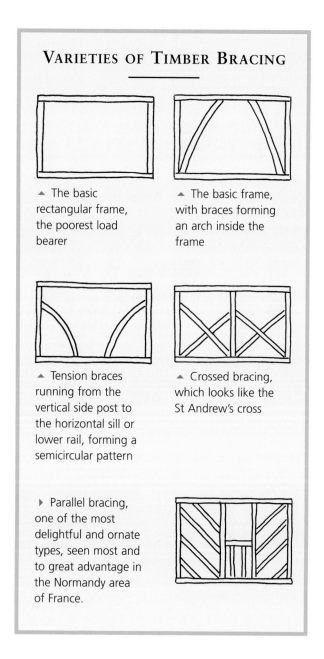

VARIETIES OF TIMBER BRACING

▲ The basic rectangular frame, the poorest load bearer

▲ The basic frame, with braces forming an arch inside the frame

▲ Tension braces running from the vertical side post to the horizontal sill or lower rail, forming a semicircular pattern

▲ Crossed bracing, which looks like the St Andrew's cross

▶ Parallel bracing, one of the most delightful and ornate types, seen most and to great advantage in the Normandy area of France.

Builders used the best materials available, lavishing most of their skill on the front of a house and using what was considered ordinary framing at the sides and to the rear, resulting in many a strange combination.

Little Moreton Hall, in Cheshire, exhibits a riot of ornate concave-sided lozenges, quatrefoils and variations including a white cross, all made by cutting and shaping upright or diagonally positioned timbers (see page 75).

LATE TUDOR HOUSE IN 1/12 SCALE

The dolls' house below is built mainly with large panels, but has small ones in the gables. By this time most houses were built with two floors, with a fireplace on each. This house has four flues (i.e. four fireplaces), all grouped around one central stack.

▲ **Larden Hall, Shipton, Shropshire, England**
This late sixteenth-century building has a simple, small-frame construction.

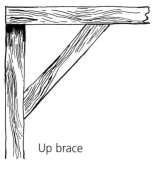

Up brace

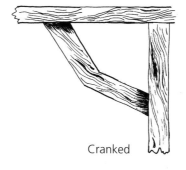

Cranked

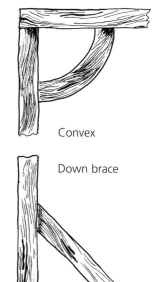

Convex

Down brace

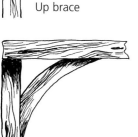

Concave

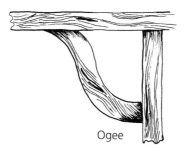

Ogee

▲ Examples of braces

Braces, which come in various shapes, make the joint between a horizontal and vertical timber stronger.

It is not clear when these came into fashion, but already in 1500 Little Moreton had quatrefoils and by 1559 they were being painted on to the plaster instead of using dressed or carved timbers.

I have drawn several variations of the intricate arrangements of braces, and so on, so that you have a visual inventory of what was available to the Tudor builder and so to you, the dolls' house builder and decorator.

▼ Hall i'th Wood, Tong Moor, Lancashire, England

An Elizabethan, panel-framed house, with ornate braces.

▶ Square panels

This mixture of quatrefoils and curved braces shows how good two types of brace can look together.

The Feathers Hotel, Ludlow, Shropshire, England
The Feathers Hotel started life in 1619 as a private house. It is one of the most ornate small houses of the period and has a wealth of two-dimensional carving, rather than the flat panels found in great houses and halls such as Little Moreton Old Hall, in Cheshire.

Haslington Hall, Cheshire, England
Close studs with up braces.

West Midlands, England
Balusters under eaves on the front of a house – a special feature of this area.

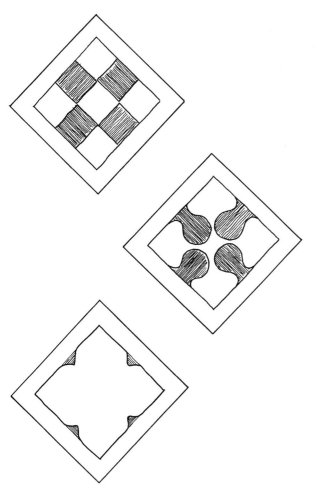

▼ **Field stones, tiles and bricks decorate a panel**

▲ ◀ **Speke Hall, Merseyside, England**
Four panels of bracing of a type entirely unknown elsewhere are to be found at the north end of the east range on the courtyard side, partly obscured by the north range of 1598.

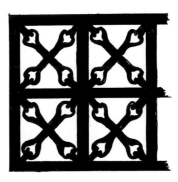

▲ **Manor of Lisores, Normandy, France**
Parallel braces and close studs.

PANEL-FRAMED CONSTRUCTION

Most 'timber-framed' dolls' houses are the traditional box construction, where timbers are applied to the outer face to simulate the timber frame. Actual timber frames, as described on the facing page, are within the capabilities of most miniaturists – you just need to have the courage to start.

Tudor builders would take a small frame of stout oak timbers and fill it with an ornate mixture of braces to create a panel-framed construction. The variations used on any one house can be numerous, and the locations and dates on the drawings in the previous chapter are intended to help you choose the correct mixture for your dolls' house. As a rule there are two or three panels to the height of one floor, so choose the grouping that looks best on your house – do mix your styles, but check that the various elements were traditional in the area your dolls' house came from.

This model hall is only the central part of a larger house, which would be built in three parts: the hall, the solar and the service wing. The hall is of two bays, that is it has two areas tied together by stout beams running from the front to the back wall.

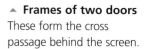

▲ Frames of two doors
These form the cross passage behind the screen.

◀ View from the front
Here you can see the cross passage.

20

PROJECT
MAKE THE PANEL-FRAMED HOUSE

Paint or stain some timbers, then build up the main framework by fixing the timbers to a plain wall. Cut the braces you wish to use from fine ply or thin wood, and lay them in the frames. Try a number of variations, but do not glue the braces in position until you have made your final choice. The result may be as simple as my drawing of Larden Hall (see page 15) or as ornate as Hall i'th Wood (see page 16).

The filling between the timbers can be achieved in various ways. On the front of the model shown left, the close studding has been filled with foam-board of the same thickness as the timbers themselves, with any cracks being plastered over.

To the back another technique was used. Panels of light wood were cut to fit each frame then various types of brace were cut and glued to them.

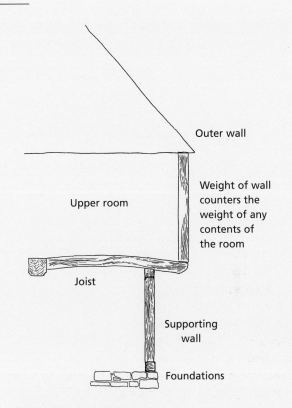

Projecting upper floor
Diagram showing how the weight of the upper wall reacts on the joist, to allow it to carry more weight.

When inserted into the frame, the front face of the braces should be flush with the outer face of the frame, while all inner surfaces are also flush. The thickness of the panel and the brace when glued together should equal the thickness of the timber frame. Plaster the depressions on the outside, to give your model that realistic look. Don't worry about marking the timbers with the plaster, as you can sand it back when dry and a little blotch here and there will make the model look more realistic.

The wings intended for this house each have two floors and one has a jetty that is the upper room projecting forward by some 12–18in (30.5–46cm) beyond the ground floor. It is only when the upper floor projects on two or more sides that you have to stop and think about the techniques used. The dragon beam, described overleaf, is the answer.

View into the house
Here you can see two completely different timber styles, which is not unusual: decorated small panels with various braces on the back, and close studding on the front which, because it was a rich man's technique, used timber of far greater quality than was necessary.

THE DRAGON BEAM

The dragon beam, which was first introduced in the fifteenth century, was much used in the sixteenth century and well into the seventeenth century. It allows an overhang to an upper floor and actually strengthens the joists due to the weight of the upper wall counteracting any contents or internal walls resting on them.

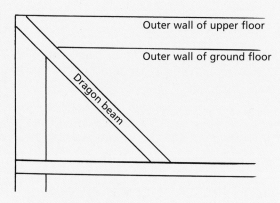

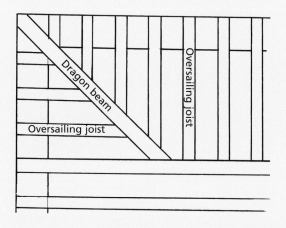

▲ The dragon beam
Method of construction, dating from the fifteenth century, which allows the upper storey to be thrust out on two sides carried on oversailing joists.

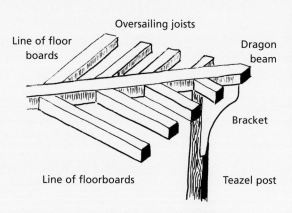

▲ Diagram of dragon beam construction
This diagram shows how the dragon beam is supported at its outer end by a corner post known as a teazel post. These posts had brackets, which could be richly carved.

▶ Dragon beam and teazel post
Corner or teazel post carrying the outer end of the dragon beam, at Wool Hall, Lavenham, Suffolk. The bracket here is part of the post, but most are applied. Next to it, and supporting the end of a joist, is an intermediate bracket which can also be seen on the house opposite.

End view of the hall with screens in place

This shows the pitch of the roof. The timber in the height of the roof was the same length as the width of the house – making an equilateral triangle – to throw off the rain. This pitch was kept even when slate roofs came in.

The fireplace and the window

The chimney breast

Once central hearths were replaced by chimney breasts there was more space inside. The chimney breast was inserted by simply cutting a hole in the wall, taking out a few panels, and putting it in. Chimneys were status symbols and fireplaces were made an internal feature. Outside the chimney stack was made prominent and dressed with impressive chimney pots, sometimes three to a floor. Any vacant space was used for a dog kennel – note the one here, bottom right.

ADAPTING A BASIC
DOLLS' HOUSE

If you prefer to start with a basic dolls' house, the following diagrams show how you can transform it into a Tudor one by adding period details (see also pp. 53–80, 'Period Details').

▸ **The basic dolls' house**

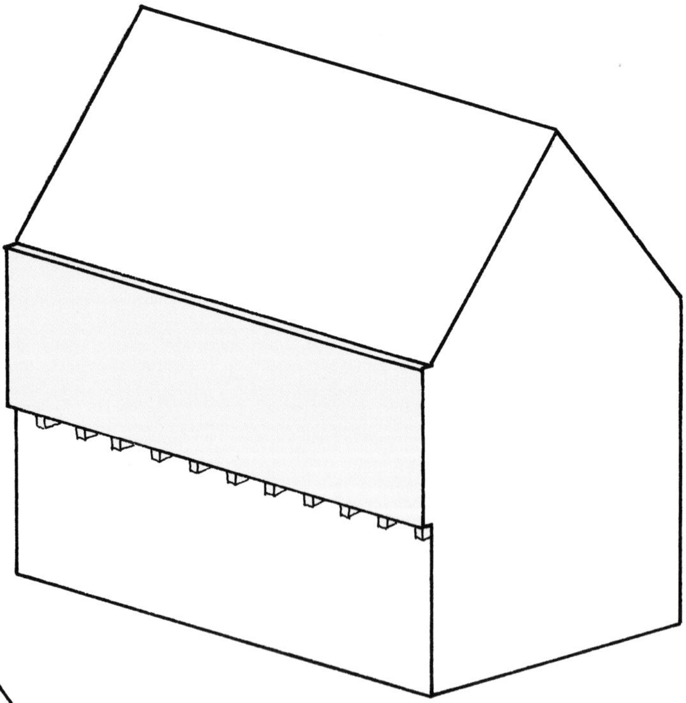

▸ **Lift your model out of the 'basic'**
Fit a panel of wood to thicken the upper section of the wall, and glue ends of 'beams' as shown. Bevel the top edge of this piece so that it fits under any overhanging roof, or continues its slope.

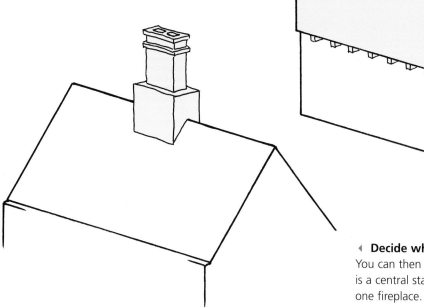

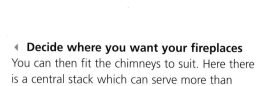

◂ **Decide where you want your fireplaces**
You can then fit the chimneys to suit. Here there is a central stack which can serve more than one fireplace.

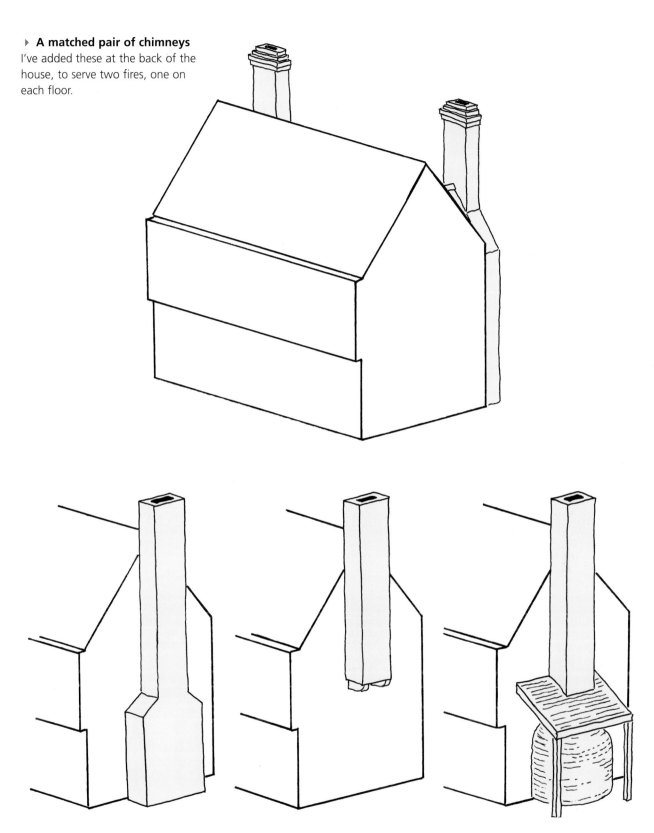

▶ A matched pair of chimneys
I've added these at the back of the house, to serve two fires, one on each floor.

▲ A simple gable-end chimney, which can be of brick or stone.

▲ Another gable-end chimney, to a first-floor fire.

▲ Ovens were built out from the base of a chimney.

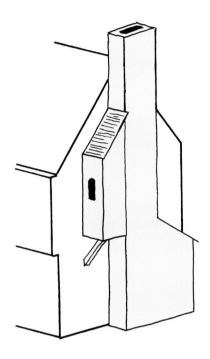

△ Garderobe
Built into the side of the chimney.

△ The basic house with a porch and an oriel window
I have moved the door, but your porch could line up with an existing door.

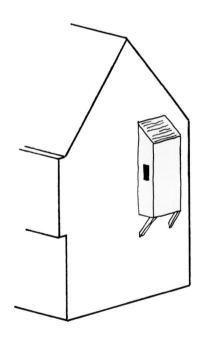

△ A projecting garderobe
Could be on any wall, even a front one.
(See 'The Cloakroom', on page 87.)

△ An indication of what can be achieved

FILLING THE GAP: WATTLE AND DAUB

The non-structural infill between the structural framework of timber-framed buildings could be one of several locally available materials: in close studding it could be blocks of wood, slabs of slate or other stone, brick, or flints, but wattle and daub was most frequently used. The wattle consisted of reasonably stout uprights of oak or hazel, which were inserted into a slot or hole in the upper cross member of the frame, then sprung into an upright position and anchored into a groove in the lower cross member. A horizontal interlace of hazel rods, riven oak, brushwood and even reeds, resulted in a hurdle set in the main timber frame of the house walls.

A coat of plaster or daub – a mixture of mud, cow hair, manure and chopped straw – was then applied to the wattle, inside and out, to make the house draught-proof. In some areas feathers, sand and stone dust were added, too. The outside face of the wattle required a harder, smoother coat of plaster than the inside one, and to weatherproof the outer face of a wall, a mixture of mutton fat and cow dung was sometimes used.

▲ ▼ **Examples of wattle and daub**

BRICK NOGGING

Brick houses were the preserve of the rich, and a material little used in the vernacular homes of the poor. Prior to this, in smaller houses, brick had been confined to modernizations, chimneys, ovens and infilling for houses with timber-framed walls.

There is evidence to show that a few houses had brick nogging from the outset, but only a few superior ones. Brick nogging was, in most instances, a secondary feature used to replace damaged or worn wattle and daub.

St Margaret's, Tilbury Juxta Clare, Suffolk, England

The rather worn wall painting, below, is on the west wall of this small church. There are fragments of fifteenth-century paintings confused by sixteenth-century overpainting, but the scene of importance to us shows a man holding a white horse, and standing in front of a fifteenth century timber-framed house with a tiled roof, brick foundations and brick nogging (in the gable, at least).

The De Vere House, Lavenham, Suffolk, England

Lavenham, arguably Britain's best Tudor village, has a wealth of period detail but the De Vere House would stand out anywhere, not only because it is one which may have had brick nogging from the outset, but because of the quality of timber used and the richness of its carving. Below you can see the herringbone brick nogging. The rows of nail-holes tell us that this house was plastered over at some time in its history, that is, it was pargeted, before the second half of the seventeenth century.

While today the term nogging is mainly used to describe brick infill, which can be most decorative, many other materials were used. The 'Old Shop', in Bignor, Sussex, is a Wealden-style timber-framed house with several types of infill on view, including flint, brick and wattle and daub. Paycock's House, Coggeshall, Essex, is a jettied house with walls of close studding and brick nogging in much the same style and quality as the De Vere House mentioned above.

▲ Kentwell Hall, Long Melford, Suffolk, England
Brick nogging in the service wing, c. 1563. The bricks are not used to decorate as in the De Vere House (left), but roughly placed to fill the gap, so there wasn't too much work cutting the bricks to size.

In Germany, which has a tradition of timber-framed construction being built over a much longer time-scale than in Britain, brick nogging was set in the timber frame in the most complicated of geometric patterns, with good examples in both town and country. In the UK brick nogging is on the whole a product of the later seventeenth century, and then only as a repair for worn out plaster. So use it with care, bearing in mind the date of your house.

In Normandy, northern France, there was a tendency to use 'wall tiles' or special bricks 10½ x 5½ x 1½in (26.5 x 14 x 3.8cm), laying them on edge, which gave a most decorative finish. Not only did they use many tiles, but also glazed bricks and dressed and undressed stone.

▶ Tile, limestone and field flints
These are at the Old Manor at Orbec, France.

COVERING THE GAP: PARGETING

The timbers of timber-framed houses moved due to the climate and became a poor fit, which allowed the elements into the house. Plastering the outside of a house was cheaper than hanging boards and, as a way of resisting the weather and making the house draught-free, this was a technique much used in older houses. However, plaster looked rather drab, so pargeting – an incised ornamental pattern – was introduced to decorate them, and so would only have been a statement of pride or boasting of one's wealth.

In the UK most pargeting on the outside of a house is secondary, it being applied to cover the timber frame, wattle and daub or other infill, in order to reduce penetration of cold winds. There are a few examples, as a rule modern, where the pargeting is made to fit between the exposed timbers. In Germany there is still today a tradition of pargeting inside the timbers.

Many inventories of the period list treasures left in a will (see page 138), including things such as 'ceilings of my hall'. These are not the ceiling overhead, but wooden panels fixed to the inside of a wall to keep out the draughts, to ceil, cele, ceal or seal by fixing wainscot or plaster. Many houses have panels which were made for another, but moved by fair means or foul.

In 1519 William Hormann wrote: '*Some men wyll have thyre wallys plastered, some pergetted and whytelymed, some roughe caste, some pricked, some wrought with playster of Paris.*'

While now pargeting is mainly found on cottages as against great houses, popes, czarinas and kings have employed it on and in their palaces in the past.

THE ANCIENT HOUSE, CLARE, SUFFOLK, ENGLAND

This building (right) proclaims in its pargeting that it was built in 1473. This may be the date of the house but the pargeting is much later and, as is often the case, is a much-restored restoration of several previous restorations. Pargeting is a vulnerable form of decoration, and none is thought to survive in Britain prior to the reign of Queen Elizabeth I (1558–1603).

Drawing of Nonsuch Palace, based on Speed's Map, 1610

Here you can see the pargeting on the outer walls and in the courtyard of this largest, and most important of pargeted buildings.

The inner court was half timbered with the areas between the timbers supporting plaster sculptures which were arranged in at least three tiers. The lower one depicted the Arts and the Virtues, and on the King's side one of the upper tiers carried the Labours of Hercules and various other gods and goddesses interspersed with royal badges and floral panels.

The Queen's side had 'heathen stories with naked female figures', while running all round the courtyard, at the top, were over 30 busts of Roman emperors, much like the ones by Giovanni da Maiano at Hampton Court (c. 1520–21). All the plaster panels were painted white then framed with carved and gilded slate. These carvings were of birds, fruit, scroll work and guilloche, or twisted ropes. The focal point seen on entering the courtyard and at the far side was a pair of statues of Henry VIII and his son Edward.

You can decorate part or all of your dolls' house using simple tools to impress or inscribe some of the patterns I have drawn on pages 33–4.

Alternatively, you might prefer to use low-relief mouldings, such as those often employed for ceiling roses or swags.

Embossed wallpapers are the easiest way to represent pargeting in a dolls' house. Glue such two-dimensional decoration in position, then prime before applying a thin coat of plaster or, much easier still, a thick coat of emulsion paint. Do remember, though, that not all plaster was white.

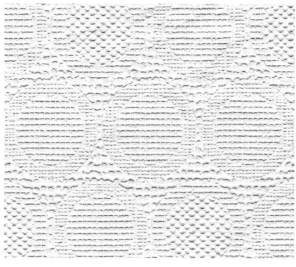

Embossed wallpaper
The easiest way to represent pargeting in a dolls' house.

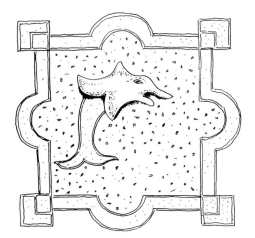

◂ **Sign of a Dolphin, Saffron Waldon, England**
Only the head is built up, the rest was created by pressing wood into wet plaster. The random scumble work was last.

The brave can achieve greater and much more personal detail by applying a good even coat of plaster, say ³⁄₁₆in (4mm) thick, which must be allowed ample time to dry and set. Draw on to this the design which best suits your house, then gently scrape plaster off to leave high points. You may wish to use templates and these can be reversed, if required, to give symmetry to the finished job.

◂ **German inscribed and impressed pargeting**
Most is later than the British work and the timber framework of the house is on view, so not used to keep out draughts.

▴ **Impressed plaster panels**

You could use a design like that on the Sun Inn, Saffron Walden, or have emblems of the trade followed by the occupant of your house.

If you cannot work direct on the face of your dolls' house, apply your pargeting to a pre-cut board and mount it in position later.

◄ ◄ Sun Inn, Saffron Walden, Essex
This has a gable with no window. The inn was much used by the haulage trade and these two fellows are thought to be a local carter, Tom Hickathrift, and a marauding giant who Tom slew using the axle of his cart.

▼ Plaster panels and friezes from East Anglia, England

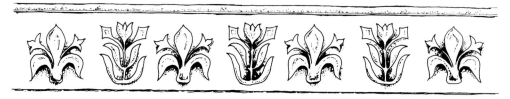

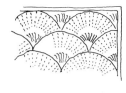

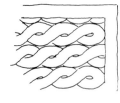
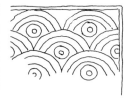
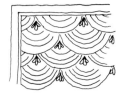

The Hazards of Fire

The Tudor builder, no matter what style or type of timber frame he used, faced one great hazard and that was fire. To overcome the problem builders came up with various ideas: the best houses were given a tiled roof, while thatch was covered with mud or lime plaster to reduce the risk factor, but they also had a little bit of superstition or magic that worked for them. The salamander, a lizard-like animal which is supposed to live in fire, or at least be able to endure it, was carved on houses of the sixteenth century as a sort of fire insurance. The golden salamander (right) is on a wall bracket on Churche's Mansion, Nantwich, while the salamander below, is a not-so-bright variation, which hangs upside-down from a house in Shrewsbury. Due to their impervious qualities, in some parts of the world, asbestos was known as salamander's wool.

The two beasts shown here give some idea as to just how few builders had actually seen a salamander.

In kitchens of the period there was a poker called a salamander which was kept hot, so that it could transfer fire to anything from a charcoal burner to a clay pipe or, in the field, to ignite the powder in a cannon. Back to the domestic front it was also a term applied to a circular iron plate which was heated then placed over puddings, and so on, to brown them. With a pedigree like that you must hang one in your kitchen, even if you don't have one on the outside of your house. If you wish to try your hand making one from polymer clay, to mount on your house, it should be about 1in (2.5cm) in length and, when finished, gilded prior to fixing in position.

▸ **Golden salamander**

▾ **Salamander**

ROOFING

Since few early roofs survive, we have to rely on documentary sources and archaeological evidence, and burnt straw, heather, or reed is often found during excavations. As early as 1212 the London Assize laid down conditions of roofing as follows:

> 'Whosoever wishes to build, let him take care, as he loveth himself and his goods, that he roof not with reed, nor rush, straw nor stubble, but with tile only, or shingle or boards, or if it may be with lead or plastered straw within the City and Portsoken. Also that all houses which till now are covered with reed or rush, which can be plastered, let them be plastered within eight days, and let those which shall not be so plastered with the term be demolished.'

Thatch is good insulation and in East Anglia early tiled roofs were set on a bed of straw or reed, and the underside plastered. Celia Fiennes recorded in her journal that every '*Holly Thursday when the mayor is sworne in the inhabitants of Norwich newe washe and plaisters their houses within and without*'. Whitewash itself was believed to be a useful fire-proofing agent when applied to thatch.

THATCHING

The word 'thack' from the old English 'thaec' (thatched) originally meant only the outer layer of a roof. Thatch roofs were made up of layers:

first a bed of hazel or willow canes, then a layer of turf with moss (or sod undercoat) in some areas, then a layer of reed, straw, rush or heather thatch, and lastly a layer of plaster or mud. Thatch was never simple or artless, but in harmony with the immediate environment and elements, and even seemingly casually erected roof timbers will be found to incline towards the wind.

A 'sod undercoat' is an archaic element, which was a good base, whatever the status of a house.

▲ **The underside of a tiled roof**
This shows the pins holding the tiles in position.

◀ **Thatch and tiles**
Two materials have been used on this roof, and it still looks good.

PROJECT
THATCHING A DOLLS' HOUSE ROOF

Various materials are used to reproduce thatch in miniature, but I find that the best results are achieved by using coconut fibre fixed to metal mesh which is the shape and size of the roof to be covered, and so this is the method I give here.

YOU WILL REQUIRE:

Three bundles of coconut fibre (for a small house)
A piece of metal mesh 3in (7.5cm) wide and as long as the ridge of your roof
A good glue (PVA, or a rubber-based one)
Curved scissors
A metal comb or dining fork

METHOD

1 Mark lines on the board forming the roof of your house, parallel with the ridge and eaves, and about 1in (2.5cm) apart.

2 Extract a small amount of coconut fibre from one of your bundles (when held between your fingers it should be about ½in (12mm) diameter).

3 Dip ¼–½in (6–12mm) of one end of the fibre in glue, then lay it on the roof along the bottom line. When positioned, it should cover about 1in (2.5cm). Repeat the process along each line in turn.

4 Glue coconut fibres across the piece of metal mesh from end to end and then, when set, stitch it down using stout linen thread in a design of your choice. If you need inspiration, look up variations in photographic publications.

5 When the thatch is complete, use the metal comb and scissors to trim any humps, bumps and tail ends to achieve the finish you require.

6 Trim neatly, then fold over the ridge, and again glue and stitch it in place.

The sods were cut from close-grazed turf, in strips 2–3in (5–7.5cm) wide and 2½in (6.5cm) thick, and could be as much as 12–14in (30.5–35.5cm) long. They were then laid on the roof, overlapping the ridge on the side of the house away from the prevailing wind, as well as overlapping laterally. Next, they were 'sewn' in turn to the purlins with ropes of traditional material and manufacture. Successive layers of thatch were secured with hazel or willow rods, which were inclined upwards, to prevent water following their line and entering the house.

Old illustrations show that not all thatch was smooth: much of it was in steps like tiles, one row set on top of the other with no attempt to smooth out the overlap.

◄ **This 1/12 scale cottage shows thatch similar to examples found in Dorset, England**
Thatched cottages were the homes of the poor, and thatch was still used by 85 per cent of builders. It wasn't until the eighteenth century that vicars were advised to replace thatch, so as to maintain their status in society.

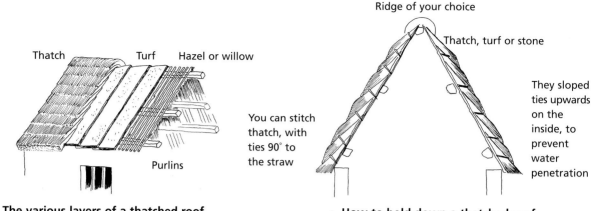

Thatch　　Turf　　Hazel or willow

Purlins

▲ **The various layers of a thatched roof**

Ridge of your choice

Thatch, turf or stone

You can stitch thatch, with ties 90° to the straw

They sloped ties upwards on the inside, to prevent water penetration

▲ **How to hold down a thatched roof**

Period illustrations show roofs of this type, but also tile and thatch mixed, and all-tile roofs. As a miniaturist, you should think of the period of your model and thatch it as it would have been, not as we do today.

Stitching down the fibres that make the ridge allows you considerable expression, and the results in real life are a thatcher's trademark. The lines that mark out the design are pliable rods called 'liggers', but I find the stout bristles of a hard broom are just right. Place them, bend them as required, then stitch them down. When you are happy with it, glue and bend it over the ridge of your dolls' house roof.

Today we are used to seeing thatch that sweeps around the angles of a roof like a well-fitting wig, but many thatched roofs required a hairnet, with ropes being used by the mile.

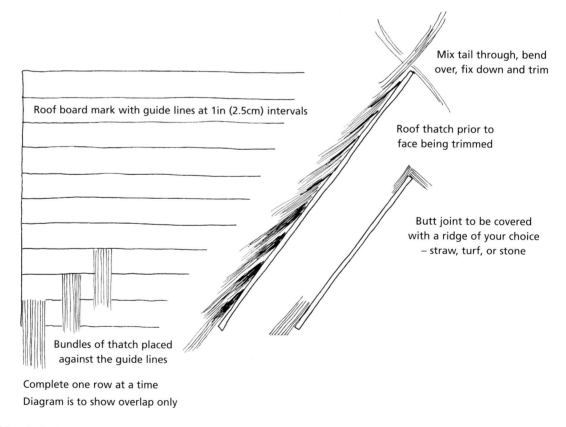

Roof board mark with guide lines at 1in (2.5cm) intervals

Mix tail through, bend over, fix down and trim

Roof thatch prior to face being trimmed

Butt joint to be covered with a ridge of your choice – straw, turf, or stone

Bundles of thatch placed against the guide lines

Complete one row at a time
Diagram is to show overlap only

▲ **Thatching techniques**

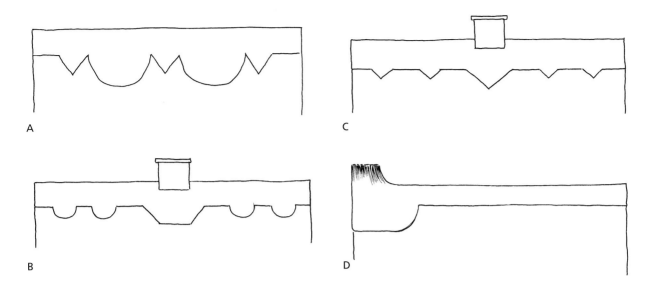

▲ **Ridge patterns for a thatched roof**
A: Scallops and points
B: Central brick chimney with scallops to ridge

C: Central brick chimney with points to ridge
D: Thatched chimney

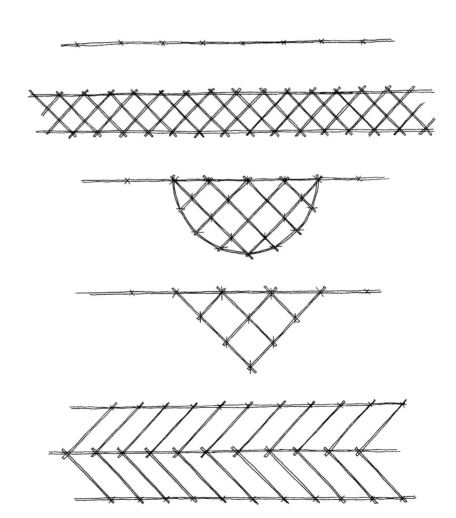

▶ **Liggers**
When these rods are used to mark out the design, they are always visible on the surface of a thatched roof so, over the centuries, they have not only held the long straw thatch firm, but have taken on a decorative role.

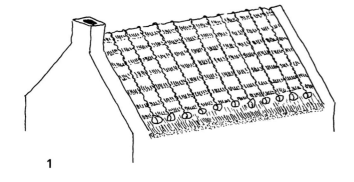

1

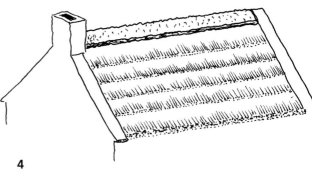

WAYS OF HOLDING DOWN THATCH

1 Roped down then rope pegged along the eaves and gables.

2 Roped down with stone weights suspended along the eaves. These weights could be above the wall head or hanging below the roof line.

3 Held down with ropes running the length of the roof, and only pegged at the gables.

4 Ridge held by pegged turf (green side up)

5 Chimney formed in the thatch.

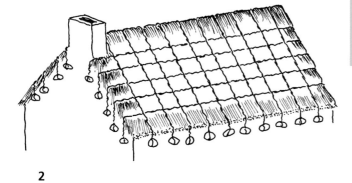

2

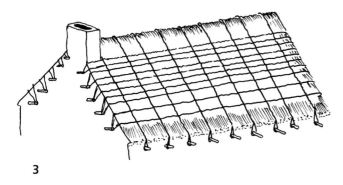

4

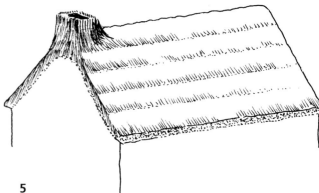

3

5

▲ **Securing thatch**

The illustrations above show some of the many ways that thatch was secured, whether on houses exposed to the Atlantic gales, or on houses in sheltered valleys.

In Tudor times, if a ceiling was required once the house was thatched, it would be formed by plastering the underside of the layer of hazel or willow canes, or by hanging heavy straw mats between the main timbers of the roof. As can be seen on the right, some of these mats preserved quite a decorative surface, depending on the material and weave used in their manufacture.

To emulate the straw mats, you could line your roof with materials such as coarse hessian fabric or coconut fibre table mats. If you want it to look as if the underside of the thatch was plastered, do not just paint the board, but roughen it a bit using plaster, then paint it.

THE INTERNAL FINISH

As important as the outside of your dolls' house is, I would hazard that you gain more pleasure from the interior, so let us look under the thatch. Most dolls' house roofs start with a flat board which is tiled, slated or thatched and the underside is simply painted, but there are more authentic things you can do with this area by giving it a period look or even a regional variation.

▲ **The underside of a thatched roof**
Here you can see the thick straw mat that supports the thatch, and also gives decoration to the room.

◄ **Vents for chimneys**
Straw thatch was not as vulnerable to fire as we think. This cottage shows little structural activity involved in the building of the chimneys, they being little more than vents.

▲ Pentice boards

Large gable ends were vulnerable to rain penetration, so were protected by 'pentice boards', which were placed along the horizontal timbers to cast the water off. Wide overhanging thatch tended to overcome this problem.

If you want to emulate a roof where the thatch is set on turf, start the internal finish by gluing miniature carpeting of a suitable brown shade on the underside of the roof.

Next, construct the hazel bed on which the turf rests and which is seen from inside the house. To do this, glue lengths of fine twigs to the carpet, placing them close together and running from the ridge to the eaves. When all of this is set and safe, glue heavier section wood purlins in position over the twigs, to hold the top and bottom, and the ends of the fine twigs, then put one piece in mid-way. For the most part these fine twigs should be left in their natural state, but for about 1–1½in (2.5–3.8cm) above the wall head they should be roughly painted to match the walls of the room.

▶ **Overhanging thatch**

CHAPTER TWO

BRICK, STONE AND PLASTER

Brickwork • Stone: First-Floor Living • Plasterwork

BRICKWORK

For some unknown reason, brick-making in England ceased with the departure of the Romans, yet in other parts of Europe the tradition continued, and fine churches and other important buildings, which had been built in the twelfth and fourteenth centuries, still remain.

England has no comparable examples, and the re-use of old Roman bricks is our only contribution. This limited source of material meant that these structures were to be found only in the vicinity of defunct Roman settlements, such as Colchester, Essex and St Albans, Hertfordshire.

At first new bricks tended to be imported, resulting in the construction of brick buildings being not far from the quayside of major ports. In 1278 over 200,000 Flemish bricks were landed from one ship alone for use at the Tower of London.

Help was at hand for the native industry, when immigrants from the Low Countries began to populate East Anglia with numbers of skilled brick-makers. This in turn led to the building of brick houses in settlements neither on a river, nor by the sea. These materials were only used in prestigious developments including schools, colleges and a few large houses such as Tattershall Castle, Lincoln – a castle in name only – which was the home of Henry VI's Lord Treasurer, Ralph Cromwell.

HISTORICAL REFERENCE

It was only in the fifteenth century that we began to call a brick a brick: in 1353 bricks were known as 'waltighel', in 1357 'flaunderstiell', in 1404 'walletiel' and finally in 1405–6 as 'brick'. Roof tiles were 'thacktiell' and roofers, for want of a better word, were 'tile thakkers', while bricklayers were 'tilewallers'.

Bricks had to be used in a uniform size, because a charter of 1571 (the thirteenth year of Elizabeth I's reign) dictated that they should be 9 x 4¼ x 2¼in (approx. 23 x 10.8 x 5.6cm). This was followed by a proclamation of 1625 (the first year of Charles I's reign) saying they should be 9 x 4⅜ x 2¼in (23 x 11 x 5.6cm) when burnt.

Also during the reign of Elizabeth I, the price of wood rose, because of diminishing supplies, and the price of bricks fell. This, together with the combustibility of wooden town houses and the advent of devastating fires in some of our major cities and towns, meant things had to change. So legislation was brought in obliging builders to use bricks in the reconstruction of their cities and this increased the demand for bricks. As a result, brick-making expanded at a pace, but the quality of bricks varied from excellent to poor. This manifests itself in many ways: you either have a brick building with a decidedly weathered look to it or later, mainly in Victorian times, refacing forming a patchwork with the old.

DIAPER WORK

The art of producing patterns on the face of a wall by using brick of a distinctive colour was introduced from France in the fifteenth century. This all-over surface decoration, with motifs arranged in a repeated pattern is called diaper work. Larger houses gained importance and were given a particular swagger by the use of diaper patterns in brick, which could not be imparted by battlements, parapets, clocks and sundials.

Continuous diamond patterns, using headers, were the most favoured and tended to give a building scale that could not be obtained by an unbroken mass of small bricks. Overburnt bricks were placed so that their ends or heads were on show in the face of the wall. Bricks, which had become vitrified by over-firing for this purpose, came in various colours, including blues, greys, purples and black, and there was little if any attempt at uniformity with any darker brick being used.

At Hampton Court, at least, some diapers were painted on, which is the ideal way for a miniaturist to get the required finish.

Materials other than brick were used, with flint and other stone being preferred to pick out the pattern. You could replicate this by gluing small pieces of some other material on to your brick wall.

A good example of a mixture of stone and brick is to be found at Hellens House, Much Marcle, Herefordshire, of 1641 (see page 80).

On many buildings, pains were taken to ensure that the pattern faded away only to reappear, but not always in line with each other, or even the same size. A point to note if looking at photographs of diaper work is that black vitrified bricks tend to reflect the light so that in many images they appear to be white, or at least not black. Also the colour of bricks used to pick out the diapers and suchlike tended to be softer at lower levels, then growing gradually darker the higher they went, which tended to give the appearance of even greater scale to a building.

Strapwork in brick was a Stuart innovation formed by unmoulded bricks projecting between ¾–1¼in (19–32mm) from the face of a wall. Importantly, at higher levels the pattern is reversed, in as much as the bricks forming the straps are recessed.

▲ Examples of diaperwork at Hampton Court Palace

▲ Little Moreton Hall, Cheshire, England
Brick was first used for fireplaces, chimneys, ovens and other modernizations, but this did not prevent the use of diapers formed by vitrified bricks.

1 — Chateau d'Auffay, Normandy
2–8 — Dovecote at Boos Manor, Rouen

Examples of diaper work on two buildings in France:

Examples of diaper work

STONE: FIRST-FLOOR LIVING

The Normans in times of trouble would retire to their donjons (fortified central towers), or keep living high above the fray. In Tudor times castles were not being built, but being modified to make homes more acceptable in polite society. Lower down the social scale and in areas of political unrest, security was still required but comfort was also important, and out of these demands, stone houses with first-floor living were built in many areas of Britain.

Away from the marginal farmland in the northern Pennines, and on richer lowland estates, better houses were built. There is a small group of fortified manor houses which includes two related by architectural style and owner. Low Hirst, Ashington, Northumberland (see pages 48–9) and Cockle Park, Northumberland, do not bristle with battlements but were designed with comfortable security in mind, their main defence being turrets built above one of the gables. The rest of each house is, for the period and location, rather light in structure.

FIRST FLOOR, EXTERNAL STAIR

Houses like the one above, in Jersey, are also found in northern France and in the north Pennines of England. Here, the archway consists of eleven stones, but traditionally a Jersey arch had nine stones. A fine door can be seen at the top of the flight of stone steps, also a window partially blocked by the steps and, beneath the landing, a square hole to allow light through to the window. The animals would have lived on the ground floor and the family upstairs in one or sometimes two rooms. The stairway is obviously an afterthought, as the first floor would originally have been reached by a retractable wooden one.

Houses in border towns were also built with security in mind, with the main living area being above the ground-floor food storage area.

HOLE HEAD, HENSHAW, CO. DURHAM, ENGLAND

On the right is a Pennine first-floor house, home to a hill farmer. The rectangular wooden stair has been replaced by a stone one. This drawing shows a much-modernized house of the same type as the one in Jersey (opposite), but here, as in all the Anglo-Scottish Borders, the animals were turned loose for security, rather than kept in the basement. The thinking was that animals held as a group were more at risk than creatures roaming the moors and, with this is mind, the original doors to the basements of these houses were too narrow for livestock to use.

ABERCONWY, CONWY, NORTH WALES

On the left is one of a type of house that used to abound in the town, with first-floor entry. It has a stout stone lower section and an upper floor of half-timber construction. There is an outer stair to the first floor which is also of stone, with only the second floor being of timber. While there are a few windows in the stone part, they are of quality, with one being an oriel window. As the external stair blocks a window, it is obvious that it was an afterthought and, like the Pennine examples, it replaced a retractable one of wood.

HIRST CASTLE, NORTHUMBERLAND, ENGLAND

Externally, Hirst Castle was 47ft 7in x 25ft (approx. 14.5m x 7.62m) and inside 38ft 10in x 18ft 9in (approx. 11.84m x 5.72m). The thickest wall was the western gable, which carried the two turrets with battlements and a walkway between them. Only the windows on the main front had hood moulds, or labels, to throw off the rain. The first-floor living area was reached by an external stair, and the ground-floor storage area by a doorway under the stair-head. The main door, on the first floor, was richly decorated with a coat of arms carved above it.

The house was demolished in 1908, but I recorded what was known of it, and also owned old pictures of it drawn by a local architect. I was therefore able to reconstruct it as it was in Tudor times (see right), with the turrets in place, the external stair on the front and Georgian windows replaced by period ones. The house would make a worthwhile project, as it has character yet the shape is a simple rectangle.

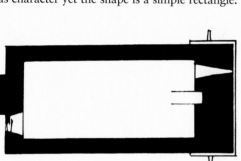

Attic area with stairs to turrets

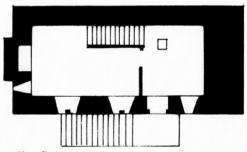

First floor with entrance at the top of a flight of stairs and a trap door to the basement

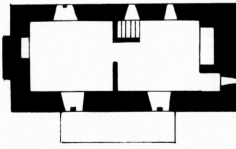

Second floor – the main living area with the best, most ornate, fireplace

For dimensions see text and page from my 'file' of drawings and field notes (opposite)

▲ **Floor plan of Hirst Castle**

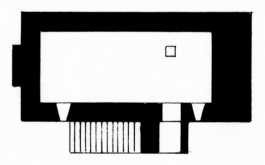

Basement with entrance under the stairs and a trap-door to the first floor

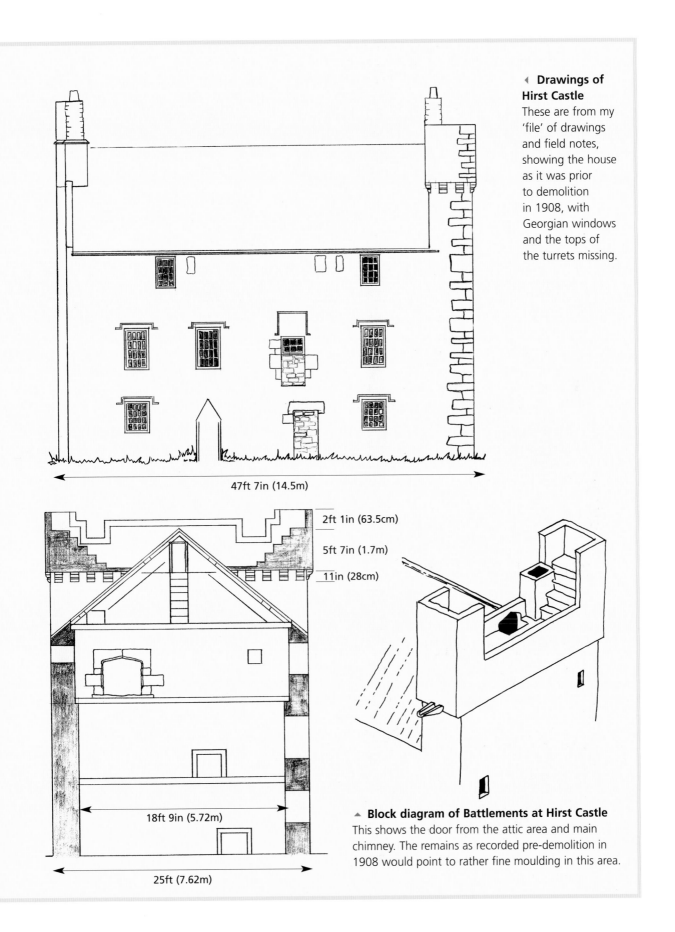

◂ **Drawings of Hirst Castle**
These are from my 'file' of drawings and field notes, showing the house as it was prior to demolition in 1908, with Georgian windows and the tops of the turrets missing.

47ft 7in (14.5m)

2ft 1in (63.5cm)

5ft 7in (1.7m)

11in (28cm)

18ft 9in (5.72m)

25ft (7.62m)

▴ **Block diagram of Battlements at Hirst Castle**
This shows the door from the attic area and main chimney. The remains as recorded pre-demolition in 1908 would point to rather fine moulding in this area.

PLASTERWORK

Much pre-cast plasterwork is available on the miniatures market, but most is not of our period, so we have to find alternatives: you could use wood mouldings meant for a cornice, small picture frames, or even buttons to make a rich ceiling. Work out what your materials will allow you to do, fix them to a board the size and shape of the ceiling to be decorated, and cover them with a thick coat of white emulsion paint. When you have the finish you require – which may take more than one coat of paint – glue it in position.

Some ceilings have fine pendants (see right), which can be built up using wood moulding and turnings such as newel posts and spindles, and finished with a thin coat of plaster or a thick coat of emulsion paint.

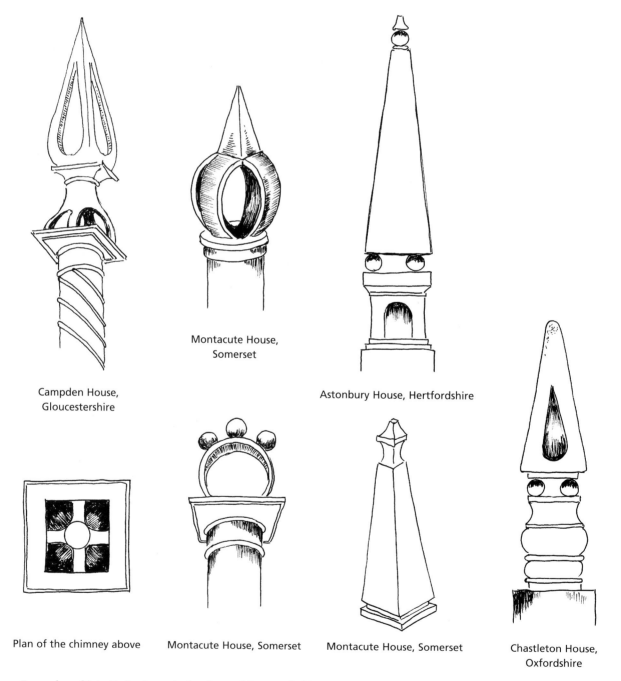

Campden House,
Gloucestershire

Montacute House,
Somerset

Astonbury House, Hertfordshire

Plan of the chimney above

Montacute House, Somerset

Montacute House, Somerset

Chastleton House,
Oxfordshire

▲ **Examples of late Tudor to early Jacobean chimneys (left) and finials (right) in England, at a time of great change**

PROJECT
MAKE A RICHLY DECORATED CEILING PENDANT

The pendant illustrated below looks most ornate, but here I show you how to break the pendant down into its main elements, so that you can build it up in stages:

1 Cut out an eight-pointed ceiling rose from card, ply, or paper clay and decorate it with an edging of fine cord.

2 Glue a cube in the centre of the rose, then bend and glue four large, stout paper 'rays' around the corners of the cube at the ceiling end, so that each ray overlaps halfway across two sides of the cube.

3 Next glue a square piece of your chosen material (slightly larger than the face of the cube) to the underside of the cube and decorate it with four small pendants, which could be cut from a spindle.

4   Glue one large pendant to the centre of this and attach a metal hook and eye from which to hang a lamp.

5 Fill any gaps with plaster or paper clay. Paint, apply decoration, then paint again.

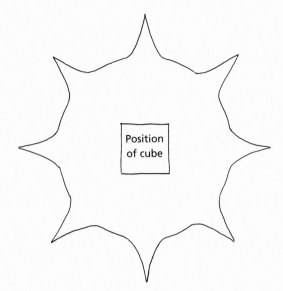

Plan view: ceiling rose in the shape of an eight-point sunburst

Section: glue rays to the corners of the cube

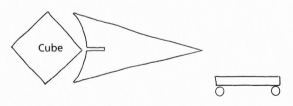

Cut four rays. Bend and glue to corners of cube. Glue one small pendant at each corner

One large pendant

Metal hook and eye for lamp

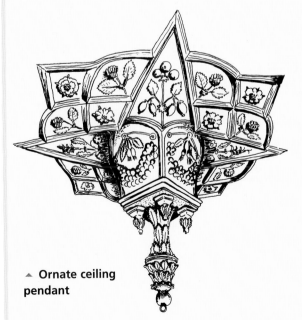

▲ **Ornate ceiling pendant**

Pendants and finials are to be found decorating ceilings, garden walls, gable ends and chimneys, and come in many forms, whether made of plaster, wood or stone. The strangest are the chimneys (see page 50). Montacute House in Somerset, and the banqueting house of Campden House, Chipping Camden, Gloucestershire, are among the best and reek of period charm, as does the lion-clasping-a-shield finial, shown below. The gardens of Montacute House have walls and gateposts which are decorated in much the same way, and any of these designs could be adapted for your dolls' house.

▲ **An ornate Tudor finial to a newel post on the main stair at Bletchley Park, Buckinghamshire, England**
Carving such detail as this is beyond most of us, but polymer clay can be used and there are miniature castings to be found.

CHAPTER THREE

PERIOD DETAILS

Doors • Windows • Shutters • Porches • Inscriptions: Make Your Mark

DOORS

We all live in a house of some sort, entering and leaving by the door, and most of us work in buildings, using the door to gain access, yet we seldom stop to look at it. The door is one of the most important elements of any building and the shape and structure of a doorway add dignity or strength to a house, and give it that period feel.

Door heads take on many shapes and, once invented, a shape will continue to be used even though it might not be the height of fashion. Semicircular arches came first, followed by the points of lancet windows and doors, which were then replaced by the depressed arch of several radii of the Tudor and Stuart periods. The flat or square-headed doorway has been with us for ever and is the type most used today.

From early times to the late seventeenth century the actual door that filled the gap was usually a simple structure made from stout oak planks. The best ones were ledged and braced, others were made of layers of planks, the outer ones being vertical and the inner layer horizontal or even diagonal. These were strong and full of character, but not refined yet. Most doors were hung on strong iron hooks and strap hinges, while others were harr-hung (see box below left).

Isolated or vulnerable houses could have two doors, one closing close behind the other, while even greater security was given by the use of an iron yett.

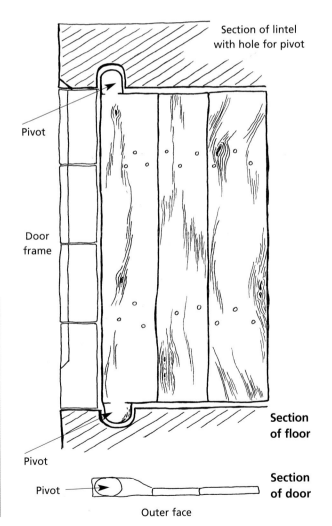

Section of lintel with hole for pivot

Pivot

Door frame

Section of floor

Pivot

Pivot

Section of door

Outer face

HARR-HUNG DOORS

Harr-hung doors are built of stout oak planks (see diagram, right). The hinge-post plank is longer than the others, and shaped at either end to form pivots that fit into round holes in the frame at the top and bottom of the doorway. They can be built into stone or timber houses.

Yetts were iron grilles, woven together in such a way that they could not be dismantled while in the closed position, so preventing the use of axes to force an entry. Like a portcullis, they could be closed while the actual door was open, giving security as well as allowing ventilation.

Late Tudor and Stuart door heads could be rich classical designs, but most ordinary houses continued to use the depressed arch with hood moulds – a projecting moulding above the arch – to carry off the rain. These hood moulds sometimes ended in ornament, even grotesque heads such as over the back door of Woolworths store in Hexham, Northumberland, shown below.

Stone doorways can be set in brick walls; indeed builders often dressed the surrounds of doorway and window openings to look like stone.

Most examples shown are from areas where stone was the local material. Doorways in timber-framed houses tended to make use of existing upright timbers with the door head set into them, which was not true of Stuart houses of this type. Again, most were square-headed, with shallow arches of various types cut into them, the lancet shape being on its way out by now.

The bottom part of most doorways was the stout frame on which the rest of the wall was fixed, so in internal and exterior doorways there is a large square timber to step over. These were known as 'thresholds' because they were originally used in barns to hold back the straw from the threshed grain. In the domestic setting, they prevented the scented rushes, and so on, used on the room floor from escaping into passages and other rooms.

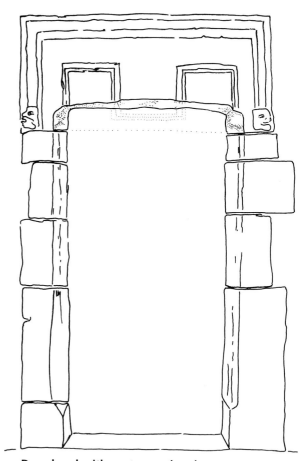

▲ **Door head with grotesque heads**

WIDE DOORS

These two photographs show just how wide doors could be – not what we now consider the correct ratio of width to height.

▲ **Weald and Downland Open Air Museum, West Sussex, England**
The door head on this square-headed door with depressed arch is based on a surviving example in a fifteenth-century building in Crawley, West Sussex.

▲ **Wearsly, Herefordshire, England**
The marks of earlier strap hinges can be seen under the layers of black paint on this fine lancet door.

WICKETS

Some doorways were so wide that the door was just too large to be moved every time you wanted to go in and out, so a small door – called a 'wicket' – was inserted in them for everyday use.

▲ **Barn Street, Lavenham, England**
This pitch-black oak door has a well-used wicket in it, used for the day-to-day passage of the household. On special days the large door would be opened.

▲ **De Vere House in Water Street, Lavenham**
This sun-bleached oak door, with an ogee-arched wicket in it, is the door to one of the homes of Edward De Vere, 17th Earl of Oxford, a leading courtier and favourite of Elizabeth I, who visited Lavenham at least once. The ornate carving shows hunters, which may tell us that it was a rich man's hunting lodge.

Ogee-headed doors
The stout one, left, is at the foot of a service stair in the courtyard of Little Moreton Old Hall, Cheshire, while the one below is in Lavenham, Suffolk. Although this one is now blocked up, the detail of its construction can be seen.

◄ ▼ **Wooden doorway and door heads in half-timbered buildings**
Most doorways of this type used existing vertical timbers to form the entrance. All are Tudor, but the lancet-type, centre bottom, would have been old-fashioned when built.

▲ **Lancet doorways left and right. The central ogee-headed doorway is from a superior, mid-Tudor period house**

DOOR HINGES

In Tudor times most door hinges were simple straps of metal with an eye, or had a folded-over end which fitted over a hook in the door frame. For the brave there was another type, and that was the wooden hinge, which was used in Monmouthshire and in parts of the Anglo-Welsh borders. The example below has double doors (the second door, not shown, is a mirror image). Each door is made up of three planks: two are thin in relation to the other, which is 3in (7.5cm) thick, and holed to take the squeak-free hinges, which are loops of hard wood tenoned into a heavy oak door frame held by tree nails or wooden pins. The outer edge of the thick plank is rounded to prevent the door jamming against the frame. There are hinges of this type in the barn from Flintshire of c. 1550 which has been re-erected at the Museum of Welsh Life, St Fagans, Cardiff.

Most metal hinges of the period, if used to hang house doors, were of the strap-and-pintel, or hook type, with only a few being of the more modern pivot and base-plate design. Base plates, the part that fits into the door frame, could be ornate but as a rule the best work was on the strap.

Medieval hinges were ornate in the extreme but by the Tudor and Stuart periods they were much less so, unless it was a palace or a church, but even they were more subdued. You can cut your own hinges from metal or card, paint them, then mount in position, even if they don't actually work.

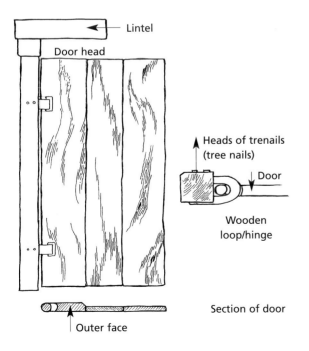

Door with wooden hinges

Lintel

Door head

Heads of trenails (tree nails)

Door

Wooden loop/hinge

Section of door

Outer face

TYPES OF HINGES

Hinges came in two types – pivot and base plate (A–B) or strap and pintel or hook (C–G). The examples here are typical of the period, although 'G' is of a special design, cranked to allow for insertion of a wicket into the main door.

A 1583

B 1598

C 1595

D 1604

E 1570

F 1591

G 1598

HALL SCREENS

Most Tudor houses were entered by a door giving on to a cross passage, then continued on out of another door and into the yard or garden, as shown in the photograph below. 'Hall' sounds grand to us, but to them it was just a type of house consisting of one large room open to the roof – the hall – with the kitchens at one end and the solar or private rooms at the other.

Early houses only had 'spurs', the part of the screen attached to the outside walls. The central area was blocked by a movable screen known as a standard. Many houses still have the spurs but few have the standard. At Rufford Old Hall in north Lancashire is just such a screen, said to be the only original one left in existence. It is a monster and only movable if you are optimistic and have strong friends. With looks of the Orient rather than Lancashire, it has eight terraced panels and three enormous pinnacles of strange barbaric shape.

Milton Abbas in Dorset has a similar transitional arrangement of 1498, with the central standard linked to the side screens by ornate ogee arches. Wortham Manor, in Devon, has screens in its early sixteenth-century hall which are little cousins of the Rufford ones. Later screens had a floor built over them which could house a minstrels' gallery but by c. 1590 at Montacute House (see below right), the screens are of stone and largely a status symbol.

CROSS PASSAGE, LAVENHAM, SUFFOLK

The cross passage shown on the left, viewed from the back door towards the front door, has the service wing, kitchens and so on, on the right and the traditional two doors to the hall on the left. This is how most houses were built. The cross passage was traditional and used for several reasons: it cut down on draught from the two doors; it reduced disturbance to occupants of the hall; and it reduced kitchen noises and smells. The wall on the left was known as the 'screen' and the passage as the 'screen's passage'.

▲ **Wooden Screens, in the Hall, Craigievar, Scotland**
These are unusual in that they have a door, but the remains of the minstrels' gallery are still to be seen at either side. The central portion was removed when the large window was inserted in 1825.

◀ **Screens at Montacute House (c. 1590)**
These are now of stone rather than wood, with fine strapwork decoration and 'fancy' capitals.

WINDOWS

Windows – or windeyes as they were known – were not to look out of, but to let light and fresh air in. Glass was new and, if you were upwardly mobile, then you just had to have glass in your windows. Alas, most of the population was not upwardly mobile, so most windows of the fifteenth to seventeenth centuries had little or no glass in them. If there was glass, it was confined to the uppermost parts of the window which would not have had shutters.

At least early in our period, most homes had an open fire in the middle of the floor, and the smoke found its own way out after visiting every corner it could along the way.

In a home like this glass was not an advantage, as a free flow of air was necessary to keep the smoke down so, when the wind was too strong, shutters were placed across the windows. These shutters took various forms, and examples still exist in many old houses; however, the best collection of shutters is to be found in the Merchants House at the Avoncroft Museum of Historic Buildings, Stoke Heath, Bromsgrove.

VENTILATION QUARRELS OF PIERCED LEAD

▶ **A two-light window at Hampton Court Palace, Surrey, England**
Within each light, there are two ventilation quarrels.

▲ **Detail of the Hampton Court window above**

▲ **Two drawings showing examples from Essex, England**

Late Sixteenth/Early Seventeenth-Century Window

Note the simple bolts and hinges in the drawing below, which is based on a contemporary painting. William Harrison writing shortly before 1587 wrote

'of old time, our countrie houses, instead of glasse, did use much lattise, and that made either of wicker or fine rifts of oke in cheker-wise … so our lattises are also growne into less use, bicause glasse is come to be so plentifull'.

Fenestrations of this kind were rediscovered when windows, which had been blocked up many years ago, were reopened. The lattice work here, which had been decorated with brass nails at each intersection, had been plastered over as if it was wattle. It was quite richly made with good quality wood. Fenestrals were even made to slide into position like shutters.

▶ TOP: A window without shutters and with glass in the upper part only.

▶ CENTRE: An area with shutters and no glass, allowing the free passage of air when required. The bottom section contains a fenestral to give light without relinquishing privacy.

▶ BOTTOM: An area with shutters and a wooden grille or fenestral, which could be covered with cloth or oiled paper for more privacy.

As late as 1815 country cottages are recorded as having lattice windows, and there are old records of the purchase of cloth for church windows.

The use of oiled paper in windows is also well documented. Thomas More mentioned it in his *Utopia* (1516) and Sir Hugh Platt in *The Jewel of Art and Nature*, published in 1594, described how to make parchment opaque for the same purpose:

> '... then straine ... the ... thinnest parchment upon a frame ... and when it is drie oil it all over with a pensil [a brush], with oile of sweet amonds, oile of turpentine or oile of spike, some content themselves with linseed oile, and when it is thorow dry, it wil shew very cleere, and serve in windows in stead of glasse ... you may draw anie persinage, beast, tree, flower or coate armour upon the parchment before it be oyled, and then cutting your parchment into square panes, and making slight frames for them, they will make a prettie show in your windowes, and keep the room verie warm. This I commend before oyled paper, because it is more lasting, and will endure the blustring and stormie weather much better than paper.'

I remember shepherds putting the skins of sheep in windows c. 1955, which prompts this question: When it was tradition to break the glass in your window to let the soul of the dead escape, was it cheaper for those left behind, and easier on the departed, to use a material you could push aside rather than break? Some glass windows catered for this, having ventilator quarrels of ornate pierced lead (see examples on page 62).

CLERESTORY WINDOWS

Some windows were never intended to have shutters and these were known as clerestory windows – not to be confused with church windows of the same name. In a domestic situation they were on any floor, as high in a room as they could be, but not tall. Their presence is an indicator of a rich interior, as they were built to light the newly fashionable carved wooden beams or the early plaster ceilings of the period.

Lavenham, in Suffolk, has numerous good examples, mostly in rooms which also have a more traditional window (see example, above). This building has a clerestory window of six lights, and two more: one between the oriel windows on the left, and another between the second oriel and the projecting porch. If the look of the house from the outside didn't say it, then these windows say 'we have a nice ceiling that looks even better with a bit of light'.

ORIEL WINDOWS

A bay window is an angular or curved projection. If curved, it could be called a bow window and if on the upper floor an oriel, or oriel window, and these were much used in Tudor and Stuart domestic architecture. When projecting from the wall face of an upper floor of a house it had to be supported on brackets, or by corbelling.

The origins of the term 'oriel' are a bit confusing, being from the Latin *oratoriolous*, a little place for prayers which was set aside in some larger apartments. The term became attached to a small closet or chamber whether it was used for prayer or not, and then it became more especially applied to a projecting window in which there may be an altar, as at Linlithgow Palace, Scotland. Even windows with sideboards were known as oriels, but nowadays it is a projecting window on an upper floor, no matter what use it is put to.

◄ ▲ **Hengrave Hall**
This oriel window over the entrance to Hengrave Hall, in Bury St Edmunds, Suffolk, is by far the finest and most ornate oriel window in Britain. Hengrave Hall was built by Sir Thomas Kytson between 1525 and 1538, and the mason was William Ponyard. The result is breathtaking – most oriel windows are much simpler than these.

▲ Henry VIII's Nonsuch Palace

This shows the fine oriel window which was above the entrance to the courtyard. It consists of three bow windows with scale-covered caps, the whole supported by multiform mouldings at the foot of the bay, with naked cherubs and coats of arms. It was demolished in 1682, but the oriel window at Hengrave Hall gives us an idea of how fine it would have been. (See also page 31.)

ORIEL WINDOW, PLAS MAWR, IN CONWY, NORTH WALES

Plas Mawr, the finest Tudor merchant's house in Britain, has a series of oriel windows supported by semicircular bases and with semicircular stone caps (see photograph and diagrams below). The lights are leaded, but not curved. You could build these as curved, using small plastic bottles to make the glass bow, or build them like the originals, cutting straight across the curve, using the diagrams below.

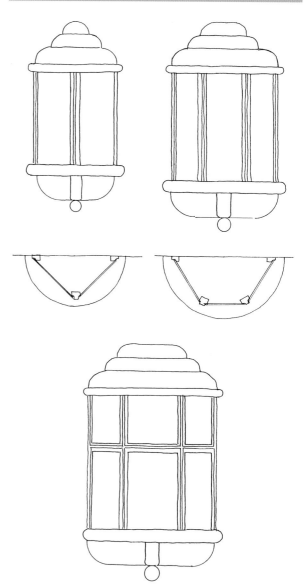

▶ **Shakespeare's birthplace, Stratford-upon-Avon, England**
This rectangular oriel window has corbelling built of two mouldings, one concave and the other convex. The roof, like the rest of the house, is red tile.

▲ **Lord Leycester's Hospital, Warwick, England**
This rectangular oriel window, with canted ends, is carried by two stout wooden brackets. The roof is almost flat, and of lead.

▲ **Selworthy village, Somerset, England**
This window is tucked into the side of a chimney – an interesting variation which would brighten any dolls' house.

SHUTTERS

Most sliding shutters ran in a groove top and bottom, but some were hung over a rail and the bottom edge was loose. The handles on shutters were simple, but came in many forms. At Great Dixter, in Sussex, there is an early Tudor two-light glazed window with a sliding shutter (see below), while at East Meon, in Hampshire, each light has its own hinged shutter with hook-and-strap hinges (shown right).

In the hall of a hall-house the shutters to the lower half of the tall window slid from side to side, but in most other houses the upper ones were hinged. In the Tudor era sash shutters were worked by hand but held up by a rope and a cleat.

A few shutters, which were used when houses were closed for the season, contained small trapdoors so that the watchman had a chink of light to guide him on his rounds. These holes were covered by a small metal grille on the outside, to keep out the birds.

Most, but not all, British shutters of the period are on the inside of the house, while in Germany they have a profusion of outside shutters.

Shutters, working or not, are one item that can be fitted to an existing dolls' house, because they do not take up much space. They can be stuck to an existing wall and, if you do want them to work, then it's not a big job, although it does take time to get it right.

▲ **Hinged shutter, with hook-and-strap hinges**

◀ **Two-light glazed window, with sliding shutter**

First floor, external shutters

England has always been a 'nation of shopkeepers', with most households having a hand in one trade or another. As already mentioned, most British shutters are on the inside of the window but here are two that open out, allowing goods to be raised or lowered from the first-floor rooms – a sure indication of trade.

Wind eyes

In the smoke-filled room below ventilation was essential, so all the windows are in fact 'wind eyes' with no glass, which let in air and allowed the wind to circulate. When less fresh air was required, the shutters – which can be seen under the windows – were raised, sliding in grooves at either side and then held up by a rope on the shutter and a cleat on the beam above the window.

◄ A removable shutter

This shutter has a pair of brackets attached to the bottom member of the window frame behind which the shutter rests. The shutter is further secured by a revolving catch or snib. When removed, the shutter would have made a good work surface, but its main disadvantage was that there were no half measures – the window was either open or closed.

▲ **Hanging shutter**

◄ **Sliding shutters**

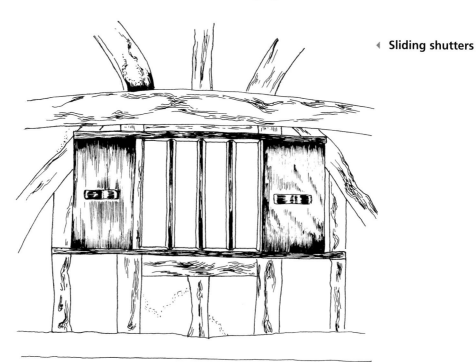

▲ Small grille in a shutter with a sliding cover

▼ Hinged shutter held up by a hook

▲ Vertical sliding shutter

▶ Hinged shutter in an upper room

This shutter is hinged at the top and kept closed using a simple catch or snib. The shutter was kept in the open position by the use of a crude wooden hook attached to one of the roof timbers.

PORCHES

Porches are that little extra that anyone can put on their house, miniature or not, to break up a dull frontage and protect the door, or people at the door. Early porches, like the one below, were quite simple and protected the door and no more, but by the time of Elizabeth I they were 'porch towers' in as much as they had as many small rooms above them as there were floors to the house. They could be built of any material and a porch of one material would be put on the front of a house of another material. So don't you worry, as long as the material you choose was available in Tudor times in the area your house comes from.

PROJECT
PORCH AT BRUNGERS FARM, TENTERDEN, ENGLAND

▸ This simple porch is made of brick and dated 1540. It has an arched entrance without a door, a stepped gable over, and in each side there is a simple two-light window. This is one to start with, and you can make it following the guidelines below.

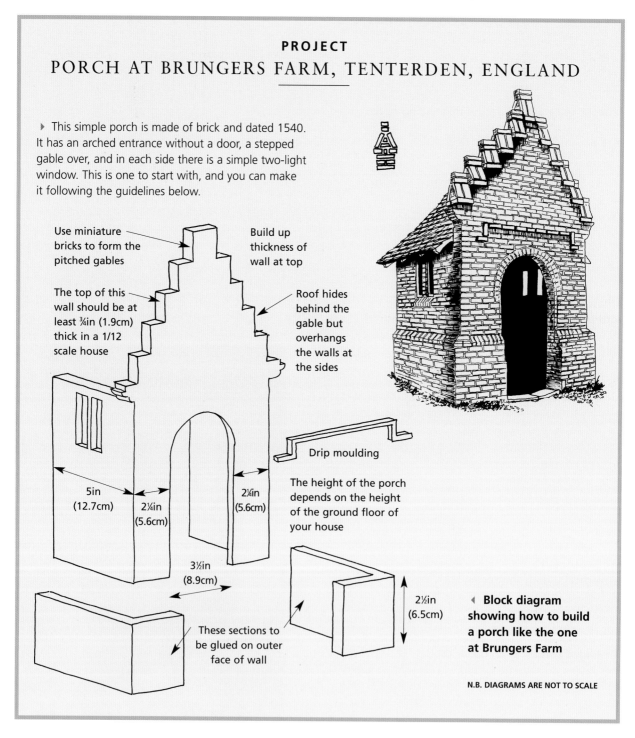

Use miniature bricks to form the pitched gables

Build up thickness of wall at top

The top of this wall should be at least ¾in (1.9cm) thick in a 1/12 scale house

Roof hides behind the gable but overhangs the walls at the sides

Drip moulding

5in (12.7cm)

2¼in (5.6cm)

2¼in (5.6cm)

The height of the porch depends on the height of the ground floor of your house

3½in (8.9cm)

2½in (6.5cm)

These sections to be glued on outer face of wall

◂ **Block diagram showing how to build a porch like the one at Brungers Farm**

N.B. DIAGRAMS ARE NOT TO SCALE

▲ **Porch Tower, Sparrow Hall, Cullercoats Northumberland, England (now demolished)**
This is another simple porch, with two small rooms above in the attic area. It is dated 1682 on the door head, a late date for such an example, although it resembles some built on early houses in America, such as Bacon's Castle in Virginia, which is also mid-seventeenth century.

PORCH AT LORD LEYCESTER HOSPITAL, WARWICK, ENGLAND

This porch (right) is little more than a small room on stilts, but it looks more complicated, as it is built on to a house with an overhanging first floor (see Project overleaf).

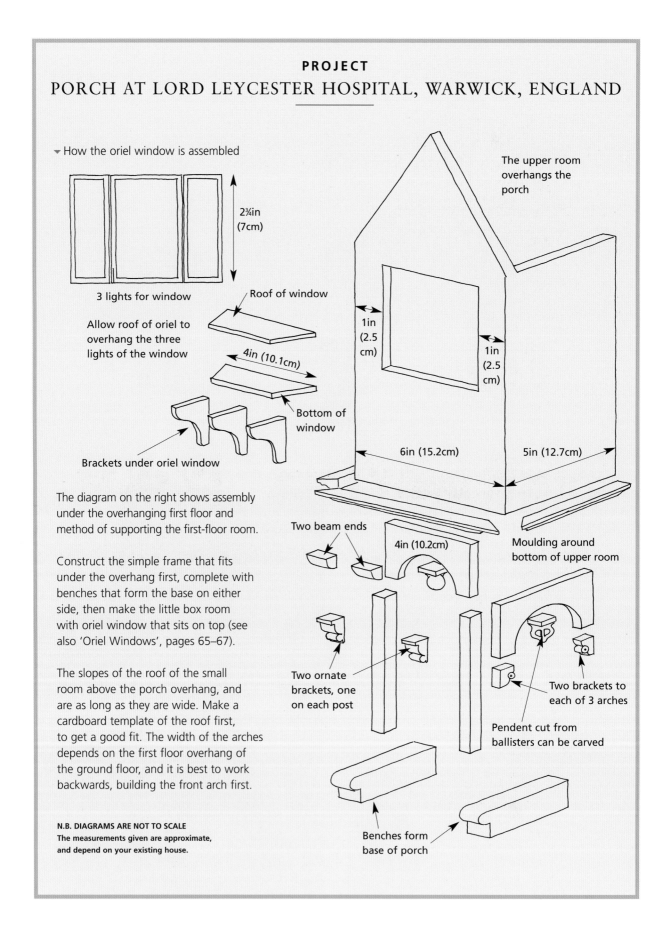

PROJECT
PORCH AT LORD LEYCESTER HOSPITAL, WARWICK, ENGLAND

▼ How the oriel window is assembled

2¾in (7cm)

3 lights for window

Roof of window

Allow roof of oriel to overhang the three lights of the window

4in (10.1cm)

Bottom of window

Brackets under oriel window

The diagram on the right shows assembly under the overhanging first floor and method of supporting the first-floor room.

Construct the simple frame that fits under the overhang first, complete with benches that form the base on either side, then make the little box room with oriel window that sits on top (see also 'Oriel Windows', pages 65–67).

The slopes of the roof of the small room above the porch overhang, and are as long as they are wide. Make a cardboard template of the roof first, to get a good fit. The width of the arches depends on the first floor overhang of the ground floor, and it is best to work backwards, building the front arch first.

N.B. DIAGRAMS ARE NOT TO SCALE
The measurements given are approximate, and depend on your existing house.

The upper room overhangs the porch

1in (2.5 cm)

1in (2.5 cm)

6in (15.2cm)

5in (12.7cm)

Two beam ends

4in (10.2cm)

Moulding around bottom of upper room

Two ornate brackets, one on each post

Two brackets to each of 3 arches

Pendent cut from ballisters can be carved

Benches form base of porch

▲ Porch Towers, Little Moreton Old Hall, Congleton, Cheshire, England

This porch is decorated with a profusion of small panels in bold black and white, with rich carved oak posts at the corners, and an oriel window seven lights wide on the top floor. One of the best and most ornate examples of the period, but the faint-hearted should not attempt to make this in miniature.

PORCH AT KEY HOUSE, CASTLE DONINGTON, ENGLAND

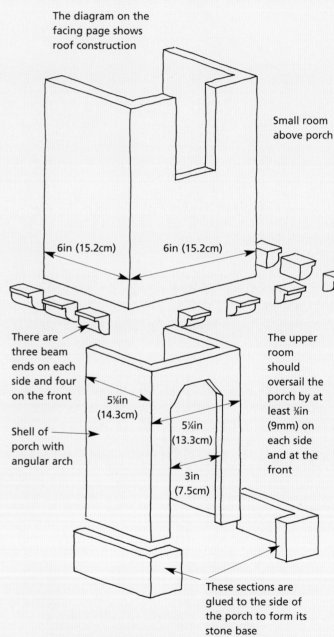

The diagram on the facing page shows roof construction

Small room above porch

6in (15.2cm)   6in (15.2cm)

There are three beam ends on each side and four on the front

Shell of porch with angular arch

5⅝in (14.3cm)

5¼in (13.3cm)

3in (7.5cm)

The upper room should oversail the porch by at least ⅜in (9mm) on each side and at the front

These sections are glued to the side of the porch to form its stone base

▲ This simple porch has confusing dates of 1595 and 1636. It was not bonded to the main body of the house, but was added at a later date. Perhaps the house was built in 1595 and the porch in 1636? The block diagram, right, shows simple boxes which could be covered/finished in any style you wish. Adjust the height of the two sections as necessary, to fit in with the height of your dolls' house. The shape of the roof depends on the shape of the roof of your dolls' house, so try this out with cardboard first.

The diagrams show how to build a porch similar to the one at Key House.

Porch roof, Key House

The roof should project forward and overhang the side walls. As a typical Tudor roof was carried on timbers as long as the room was wide, the gable end should be an equilateral triangle.

This back angle depends on the roof of the main part of the house. If fitting onto a flat wall the back slope will be the same as the front. Experiment using card first

Top of window in line with top of side walls

N.B. DIAGRAMS ARE NOT TO SCALE

Porch, at The Guildhall, Lavenham, England

This richly carved porch has one-and-a-half rooms above it. The room on the first floor has a six-light oriel window, while the half floor, in the attic, has a small two-light window.

INSCRIPTIONS: MAKE YOUR MARK

Stonemasons put their own mark on stones they had carved or dressed, not so much in pride, but as a way of being compensated for their work on pay day. Carpenters marked timbers of houses to ensure that they were assembled in the correct order, but every now and then one of their number was recognized for some special achievement, as shown on Little Moreton Hall (below). Dates such as the one on this building have to be looked at with care, as they may only refer to the building of that one element, like the bay windows, and not the complete work.

The old Manor of Orbec, Normandy, France, which is known to have been built in 1568, has a simple inscription, dated 1476, roughly carved in woodwork: 'A carpenter by the name of Thomas Le Coutelier built this fine house MCCCCLXXVI'.

LITTLE MORETON HALL, CONGLETON, CHESHIRE, ENGLAND

The inscription above, in a panel over one of the rather fine ground-floor bay windows of Little Moreton Hall, Cheshire: 'RYCHARDE DALE CARPEDER MADE THIES WINDOVS BY THE GRAC OF GOD'. His master who had paid for them had inscribed above the first-floor windows 'GOD IS AL IN AL THINGS THIS WINDOVS WHIRE MADE BY WILLIM MORETON IN THE YEARE OF OURE LORDE MDILX [1559].

▲ **Palace of Huntly, Aberdeenshire, Scotland**

Other inscriptions record not only building projects but celebrate special events, so that high up on the Palace of Huntly, Aberdeenshire (see above), George Gordon announces his elevation to Marquess in 1599 by building a series of oriel windows, two storeys high, with the following two-line inscription: 'GEORGE GORDOUN FIRST MARQUESS OF HUNTLIE' and below that 'HENRIETTE STEWART MARQUISSE OF HUNTLIE'.

Castle Ashby, Northamptonshire, was begun in 1574 and has at the top of its walls a lettered balustrade of the early seventeenth century. But you will require to put your Latin hat on. That on the outside of the entrance range and above the long gallery says 'DOMINUS CUSTODIAT INTROITUM TUUM' (May the Lord watch over your entrance).

On the inner side facing the courtyard is 'DOMINUS CUSTODIAT EXITUM TUUM' (May the Lord watch over your exit). This is grand indeed, but on the other three sides of the courtyard a balustrade of c. 1624 has lines from Psalm 127: 'NISI DOMINUS CUSTOS CUSTODIVERIT DOMUN FRUSTRA VIGILAT QUI CUSTODIT EAM. NISI DOMINUS AEDIFICAVERIT DOMUN IN VANUM LABORAERUNT QUI AEDIFICANT EAM 1624'. (Unless the Lord guards the house, they watch in vain who guard it. Unless the Lord builds the house, they labour in vain who build it.)

Less grand, the fine Tudor mansion of Felbrigg Hall in Norfolk, c. 1600, has an E-shaped entrance front with an inscription in three parts above the arms of the 'E', which simply reads 'GLORIA-DEO IN-EXCELSIS'.

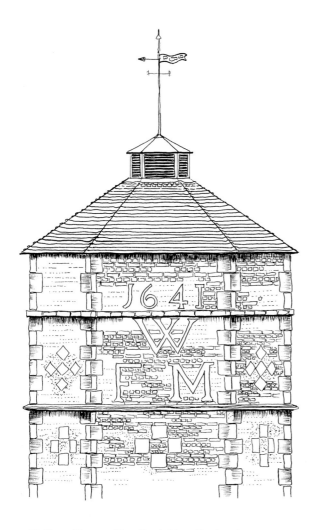

▲ Hellens House, Herefordshire, England
Here, the garden walls and ornamental outbuildings were 'marked' as well as the house, and the dovecote, which is brick-built, has the inscription and other decoration in contrasting stone.

Temple Newsam, just outside Leeds, in the West Riding of Yorkshire, has an inscription which was restored, renewed or replaced in 1788 saying: 'ALL GLORY AND PRAISE BE GIVEN TO GOD THE FATHER THE SON AND THE HOLY GHOST ON HIGH, PEACE ON EARTH, GOOD WILL TOWARDS MEN, HONOUR AND TRUE ALLEGIANCE TO OUR GRACIOUS KING, LOVING AFFECTION AMONGST HIS SUBJECTS, HEALTH AND PLENTY BE WITH THIS HOUSE.'

Most of us have not got that kind of space on a dolls' house, but please do mark your house in some special way, such as the simple initials 'ES' for Elizabeth Shrewsbury, better known as Bess of Hardwick, on the tower balustrades of Hardwick Hall, Derbyshire.

DATES OF INSCRIPTIONS

The table below shows that there was a fashion for large inscriptions, including those on balustrades, from the late Elizabethan to the Jacobean period.

Little Moreton	1559
Orbec	1568
Castle Ashby	1574
Hardwick Hall	1590
Palace of Huntly	1599
Felbrigg Hall	1600
Temple Newsam	1630

CHAPTER FOUR
LIGHT AND WATER

Lighting • Sanitation and Garderobes • Baths

LIGHTING

Candles, one of the earliest solutions to the problem of lighting the home, have been around since 3000 BC, but it was probably the Romans who introduced them to Britain. Until the introduction of gas lighting, the candle was the main source of light.

Only the great and wealthy used candles at first but, by the mid-sixteenth century, most homes had them in one form or another. The simplest was the rush light.

RUSH LIGHTS

Rush lights were made, along with their metal holders, by the householder and local craftsman. Each rush gave off a rather meagre light for as little as 15–20 minutes. Unlike fir candles, they did not have natural oils to help them burn, so had to be coated with animal fat by using a grisset. Grissets were found by the fire in all houses of the period, invariably being an elliptical pan or bowl with a handle 11–18in (28–46cm) long projecting from one of its long sides. At each end of the bowl there was a foot or short leg, and the end of the handle was also bent down to give support, like a third foot.

Waste cooking fat and remnants of tallow candles were melted down in the long bowl then the pith of a rush was drawn through the molten mass and, when cooled, stored in a special box with a number of grooves cut in it. This simple artefact is one of many everyday items you can make for your house as no two would ever be the same. To complete the set, a small iron bill hook – which was used to harvest the rushes required – would be at hand, even hanging on the wall. Hanging versions worked on a ratchet just like pot hooks of the time. The one below is metal, but there were many wooden ones.

▾ **Rush lights and candle holders**
These simple devices would be found in most houses and outnumber the fine pewter ones we tend to use. Two (left) are for use on a table while the other two (right) have spikes allowing them to be driven into a beam or a joint in a stone or brick wall. The rush was held in place in the jaw simply by the weight of the moving jaw, which often had a candle holder on it. Even candle holders were, in many situations, little more than a large nail or spike with the candle socket forged out of one end.

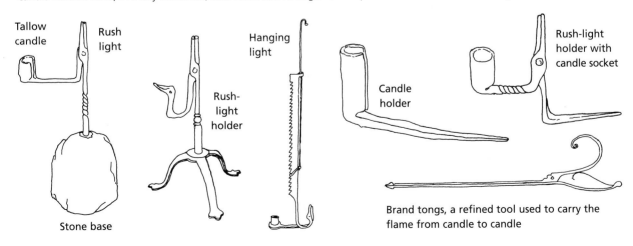

Tallow candle

Rush light

Hanging light

Rush-light holder

Stone base

Candle holder

Rush-light holder with candle socket

Brand tongs, a refined tool used to carry the flame from candle to candle

If, when reading period literature, you come across a reference to a watch light, or a night light, they were used in the same way as the rush light mentioned on the previous page. Watch lights had a longer burning time, but a poorer light, due to the way they were made. The pith of a rush light had one strip of the outer sheath of the rush left on it to prevent it breaking. A watch light had two strips left on it.

It hardly matters at scales of 1/12 or less but it is nice to know what they are talking about. Rush lights can be made from lengths of cotton thread (white) 12–18in (30.5–46cm) long (but some were 24in/61cm) and coated in PVA glue to make them rigid. If you are looking for even greater detail, draw one or two green lines along the length to represent the strips of outer sheath.

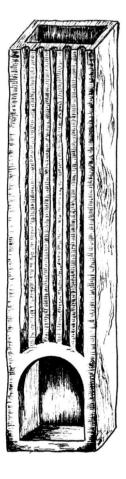

◀ **Rush-light box**
Boxes like this protected the fragile rush light.

The Greeks illuminated their dark houses using tallow and the superior beeswax candle. In Roman Britain tallow and beeswax formed the basis of all candles, with wicks made from vegetable material and, as late as 1350, these were made by the same chandlers. Just prior to the Tudor period they were separate trades. The tallow chandlers were incorporated in 1462 and the wax chandlers followed in 1483, being purveyors of superior *'Torches, Prickets, Great Candles and any other manor of wax chandlery'*.

TALLOW

Strained animal fat, free of membranous matter, was known as tallow, and was rated according to the animal from which it was produced:

- Cheapest was the foul-smelling and smoky pigs' fat
- Cheap candles were also made with beef tallow
- A mixture of beef and mutton produced a better grade
- She-goats and billygoats produced a tallow much prized for the hard gloss it gave to a candle
- Beeswax candles were the best and in 1663 Samuel Pepys tried them 'to see whether the smoke offends like that of tallow candles'. It did not
- The last type to be introduced were spermaceti (made from whale blubber), but these didn't reach Britain until the early eighteenth century

THE PEERMAN

If your house was in an upland area then light would be provided by lengths of fir from ancient bogs and cut into long slim splints, 12–36in (30.5–91.4cm), and held in a special piece of equipment known as a 'peerman' or 'puirmen', being a dialect term for a 'poor man'. Travelling tradesmen and poor vagrants would tend to the lights of anyone offering them a bed of straw for the night, and eventually gave the special light holder its now accepted name of a peerman. The burning 'fir candle' was held in the peerman by a simple spring, while the rush light was held in position by the weight of the moving jaw of the pliers-type grip. By and large the peerman and fir candle were obsolete by the nineteenth century.

▸ **Peerman with candle holder**
This example stood on the floor and is known as a 'corner peerman'. The fir candle was held in the loop of metal by the long, single leaf spring.

WALL BRACKETS

When visiting period houses most wall brackets are overlooked in the belief that they are corbels for some now lost elaborate roof timbers (see examples overleaf), yet on closer examination the remains of metal spikes used to impale candles can be found on their upper surface. Wall brackets held candles within the house, and most were built in. Many brackets are to be found as part of the fireplace, with one being mounted either side of it. While this type of fireplace, and its brackets, were going out of fashion in Elizabeth I's reign, many were built prior to that.

Bordeaux House, Vale, Guernsey, has two fireplaces with candle-shelves on either side. Those in the kitchen have hungry heads with wide open mouths ready to eat anything the cook can provide. Upstairs in the bedroom, which is a place of rest but was also associated with fertility, the shelves rest on a phallus; so you can choose your own theme, so long as it is socially acceptable.

It is easy to make brackets simply by cutting short lengths of suitable wooden moulding, painting or staining and fixing in the required position. To be truly authentic, fix one or two metal pins in the upper surface to hold the candles.

▸ **Church House, Gloucester, England**
An extremely fine candle/lamp recess.

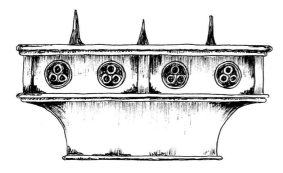

Tickenham Court, Somerset – these could be mistaken for corbels.

Side view

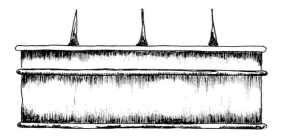

Norrington Manor, Wiltshire.

Side view

LANTERNS

Lanterns were portable lights for outdoor use and seldom used in the house. They could be of wood or metal construction, with horn, mica, or – in a few instances – glass windows. Not usually for use indoors, they had handles to carry them, or a hanging mechanism. Medieval writers from time to time refer to 'talc' lanterns which were lanterns with mica windows. Elegant examples of lanterns of all types are found in contemporary manuscripts and book illustrations.

c. 1500. Metal with horn windows and handle.

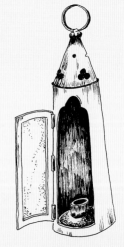

c. 1450. Metal with horn windows and handle.

c. 1503. Wood with metal rods and door, and windows of horn. Hung on a chain.

c. 1550. Wood with no windows? This must have been hung or standing in a draught-free place in a house.

c. 1400. Metal with horn window in hinged door. The loop at the top would be too hot to handle so it must have been hung.

CRUSIE LAMPS

Crusie lamps are found in most coastal areas where fish oil was available for use as a fuel. The earliest examples had a single pan or 'valve' which was used from at least Saxon times until the nineteenth century. Somewhere in Scotland at the end of the sixteenth century and start of the seventeenth century a second valve was introduced, not to give more light, but to prevent the warm oil creeping over the side of the upper valve from falling on the furnishings or floor. Simply put, the lower valve was now a drip tray. Most British examples are quite simple functional items while many continental ones are more ornate. If you compare the Spanish crusie lamp (overleaf) with my drawing of a North British ram's-horn type (below), you will see that the latter is ornate for this part of the world.

In a nutshell, the lamp – or at least the bottom valve – was hung by a hook where light was required. The upper valve was hung inside and above the lower one by way of a curved projection with grooves, or teeth, along its upper edge. The upper valve could then be tilted forward by stages to ensure that the diminishing oil supply would run forward to the hemp, moss or rush wick.

So if you hang a crusie in your dolls' house, what else would you require to service it? A supply of oil in a jug or stout jar, and a box of wicks.

The area of use was wide, being all coastal regions, and in Britain alone they had several names. In the Shetlands and Western Isles and even the Channel Islands it was known as a 'collie', while in remote Cornwall it was a 'chill'. Some areas used the terms 'cresset lamp' or 'crasset' to identify it but most, if not all, would understand and use the term crusie.

▾ Crusie or fish-oil lamps
The drawings show this simple 'two-valve' oil lamp, it being only one of many regional variations. This particular one would be found near the coast of northern England and Scotland. The hooks were fashioned so that they hung on a peg or had a spike which could be driven into a beam or a joint in a stone wall.

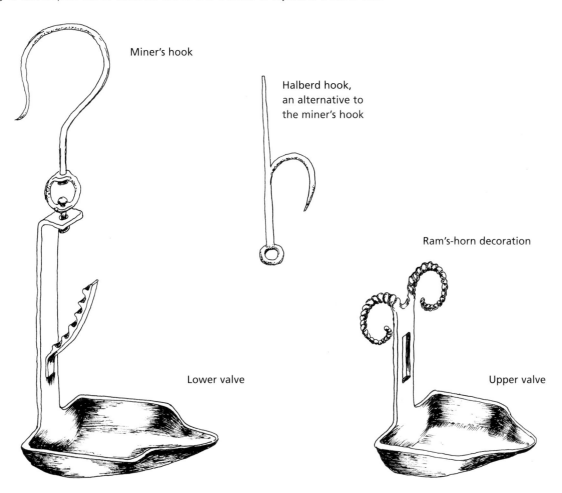

Miner's hook

Halberd hook, an alternative to the miner's hook

Ram's-horn decoration

Lower valve

Upper valve

CRESSET STONES

Side by side with the crusie lamp the simple 'cresset stone' was used, where more light was required, until at least the end of the seventeenth century. It was simplicity itself and had the advantage that the intensity of light could be varied by using as few or as many of the available fonts as were required. It had the great disadvantage that it was dirty to use. While we know it as a cresset 'stone' and most were of stone, many were made from brass or bronze, too. You could easily make a variation of this using paper clay, polymer clay or even wood, then painting it as required.

▲ **A Spanish crusie**
Behind a grille, it lights the end of a long, dark cloister.

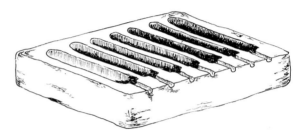

▲ **Cresset stone**
A simple lamp, 7½ x 5 x 1½in (19 x 12.7 x 3.8cm), with seven valves for fish oil and seven wicks.

LIGHTING YOUR DOLLS' HOUSE

I think that indirect lighting – which is tucked behind beams or out of sight in some corner – is the best way to light a period dolls' house and show its authentic fittings.

The Tudors and Stuarts did not hang lights as we do, but used them where and when required, with permanently placed fittings in traditional positions. Consider mini-strip lights and small spotlights as a lighting source, with portable non-electrified miniatures positioned here and there.

When I was a child 'the' oil lamp was not ignited until it was too dark to read. It was then positioned on a table which we children sat at to read, write and play games by its warm, dim glow.

Often we just used the light of the fire, as I am sure the Tudors did – you don't require candles to chat, play musical instruments and sing folk songs. It was by the fire that the history and development of lighting began.

SANITATION AND GARDEROBES

THE 'CLOAKROOM'

In the English language there are, and always have been, many euphemisms for this, some of which are of ancient origin. The word 'lavatory' is derived from terms for a small reservoir or cistern, where the religious washed to spiritually cleanse themselves: the 'lavor', a metal water jug, the 'lavarso', a ritual washing place, and the 'lavatorium' where the monks washed their hands. Perhaps the strangest is 'garderobe' from the French *garder*, 'to keep and robe' being a storeroom, wardrobe or armoury and by extension a private room. Today we still go to the cloakroom, the bathroom and the washroom, all necessary rooms. Necessary rooms of this sort were known in earlier times as the 'necessarium' and in some areas of Britain this has come down to us as the 'netty'.

While necessary, these facilities were not always private and are to be found in large numbers in ancient houses, castles and monasteries. Set in the thickness of stout stone walls, they had a seat of wood or stone which gave on to a vertical shaft, known as 'the lang drap' which discharged its contents down the outside of a building into a moat, river or special removable container, along with the kitchen waste. The content of this container was from time to time spread on the fields to fertilize the soil.

These garderobes, projecting as they did beyond the walls of a house, were cold and draughty places, but in some houses they were built into the sides or back of a stout chimney. While lots of garderobes still exist, most houses of the period show no evidence of one, and it was quite normal to urinate in a fireplace or against a wall which resulted in all sorts of household rules to control the problem.

In her book, *Temples of Convenience*, Lucinda Lambton quotes how in 1259 a Jewish gentleman from Tewkesbury fell into a privy pit on a Saturday and out of respect for his Sabbath no one was permitted to rescue him. The Bishop of Gloucester forbade anyone to pull him out on Sunday, his Sabbath, and by Monday he was dead. There is an old saying that projecting loos were, like London Bridge, for wise men to go over and fools to go under.

PROJECTING GARDEROBE WITH CESSPIT BELOW

Even town houses had projecting garderobes but, if not kept in good order, they could be a death trap. This drawing (above), after a print in a fifteenth-century translation of Boccaccio's *Decameron*, depicts a hapless man who has fallen through the rotten floorboards of his projecting garderobe into the cesspit below.

SOMETHING TO HIDE

The close stool – a chamber pot enclosed in a stool or box – was, for the period, a bit over the top. It was only used by those of a delicate disposition, or by royalty.

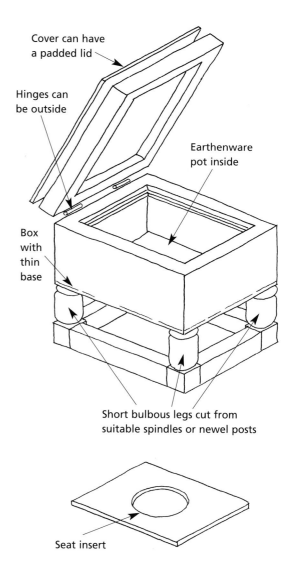

Cover can have a padded lid

Hinges can be outside

Earthenware pot inside

Box with thin base

Short bulbous legs cut from suitable spindles or newel posts

Seat insert

▲ **Close stool of c. 1600, Plas Mawr, Conwy, north Wales**

▲ **Crimson velvet 'stool of ease' at Hampton Court**
This simple box-like stool, covered in velvet which was held in place by 2,000 gilt nails, was made for Henry VIII, c. 1600. His daughter, Elizabeth I, and her successor James VI of Scotland and I of England used the same type of stool, also covered in crimson velvet.

THE CHAMBER POT

The father of the chamber pot was the medieval 'original', made of anything from glass, glazed earthenware and occasionally metal, whether tin, silver, pewter or copper. Old pots of all sorts, without being expressly made for the purpose, were used.

The first English earthenware chamber pots were roughly made and tended to be glazed, on the inside only, with thick yellow or green lead glazes. A single handle is a clue that it is a chamber pot, although many had two and some had none at all.

The Museum of London has a fine collection, including Tudor greenglaze and Jacobean ones with white slipware decoration. The content of these pots was thrown out of the window and into the street, along with the contents of the slop pail. This continued well into the eighteenth century when Jonathan Swift wrote a description of a city shower:

'Filth of all Hues and Odour, seem to tell.
What street, they sail'd from, by their sight
and smell.'

Most stools were used openly without further disguise, but with greater comfort and with the aid of a full retinue of servants the close stool would follow the sitter around the house.

The French thought they had something to hide, with Louis XI having a tent-like structure built to cover his stool, followed by his friend and ally James V of Scotland who had a green damask to mask his. The example left, based on one at Plas Mawr, has a padded lid, and you could add one to yours, too.

I hope my drawings and photographs will encourage you to fit your house with suitable toilet facilities, or to make a close stool to tuck in a corner of your dolls' house. A chamber pot can be made from polymer clay, or you can simply paint a white one brown, then paint the inside and rim green or yellow to replicate a Tudor one.

▾ **Bayleaf Farm, Weald and Downland Museum, West Sussex (reconstructed)**
A projecting garderobe with a cesspit below. This is the simplest form of garderobe to attach to a dolls' house.

THE LATRINE – 'REBUILT' C. 1568 – LE VERGER, NORMANDY, FRANCE

Apart from the window, the simply constructed half-timber projection below is similar to the one at Bayleaf Farm (left). As it was a new and exciting fitment, it was in the area of the house used by the owners as their parlour chamber, or private withdrawing room.

This type is, as the drawings shows, quite simple to construct but you will need to cut a hole in the wall of your house to give access to it. This hole could be an enlarged window opening, or a purpose-made one.

At this time there was no such thing as a toilet roll, so people used soft cloth, wet sponges, lambswool, grass or sand, depending on their status and where they lived. That is to say they used whatever local material came to hand. So you can provide your dolls' house occupants with any of the above, kept in a wooden box or earthenware container.

Most Tudor houses did not have inside toilets because they were, by and large, a new idea. With this in mind, any garderobe you attach will not have to be of identical materials: the roof can be tile while the house is thatch; the actual tower, housing the garderobe can be half timber, even on a stone-built house, or it can be rich Tudor brickwork. The choice is yours.

The Little Moreton type shown right and could be made as simple as you wish, be it half timbered as in the original, or a brick construction.

To fit a garderobe tower of this kind would require two doors on each floor – quite a feat of engineering. If you missed out the central partition then only one door per floor would be required and the occupants could hold hands while engaged.

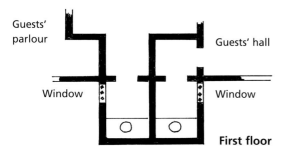

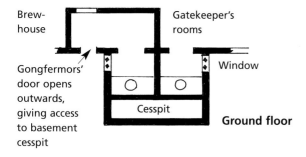

▲ **Diagrammatic layout of Little Moreton Hall Garderobe Tower**

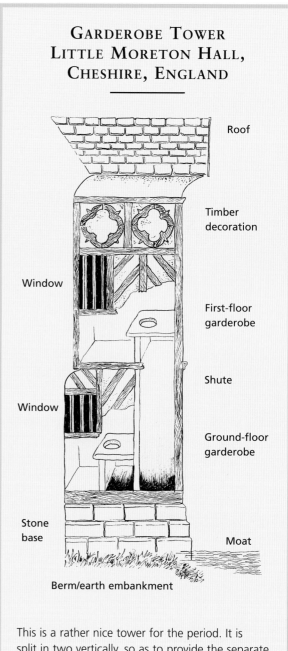

GARDEROBE TOWER LITTLE MORETON HALL, CHESHIRE, ENGLAND

Roof

Timber decoration

Window

First-floor garderobe

Shute

Window

Ground-floor garderobe

Stone base

Moat

Berm/earth embankment

This is a rather nice tower for the period. It is split in two vertically, so as to provide the separate and private garderobes on each floor, each with its own door. You may wish to have a single garderobe on each floor or a 'two seater' on each floor. Whichever you choose, they will only require one door on each floor. The stone base, which opened on to the moat to allow the waste to flow into the moat, also had an entrance for use by the gongfermors, whose job it was to shovel out the waste when the cesspit was full.

The three-tier example below, which is based on one at the Chateau de Grandchamp, Normandy, is complicated but only requires one door per floor as the first floor and attic floor only have one garderobe each and the ground floor has a friendly two-seater.

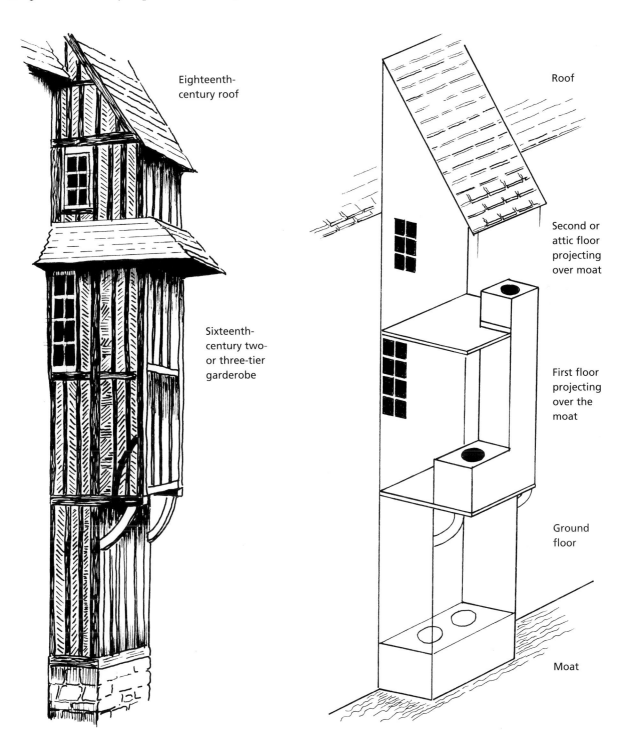

Eighteenth-century roof

Sixteenth-century two- or three-tier garderobe

Roof

Second or attic floor projecting over moat

First floor projecting over the moat

Ground floor

Moat

▲ **Chateau de Grandchamp, Normandy, France**
This tower has three floors and a slightly complicated form of shutes, allowing or directing the waste to the moat below.

▲ **Diagram of the sixteenth-century three-tier garderobe at Chateau de Grandchamp**

THE PRIVY

A privy is apart from the rest of the house, private. In fine houses, which most dolls' houses tend to be, the privy had an adjoining room to wash and re-dress yourself in. It may also have housed spare clothes and was known as the wardrobe, while the word garderobe was one of the many euphemisms for the privy itself.

LANGLEY CASTLE, NORTHUMBERLAND, ENGLAND

Interior of a garderobe tower and section of the same (right). This castle is now a hotel and the garderobe tower, with its 12 niches in three sets of four, is the main stairwell. The section shows how the shutes of the garderobes are positioned in front of each other, and how they drop to the cesspit at the bottom. This layout did not change for hundreds of years.

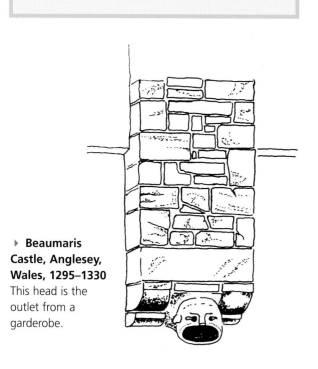

▶ **Beaumaris Castle, Anglesey, Wales, 1295–1330**
This head is the outlet from a garderobe.

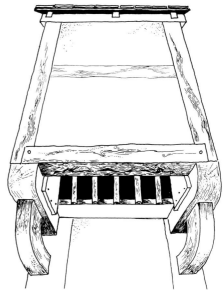

▲ **Garderobe from below**
These could be housed in any outshot or overhang of a half-timbered Tudor house. Based on a reconstruction at the Weald and Downland Museum, West Sussex.

WASHING FACILITIES

▶ **Drawing after an early sixteenth-century woodcut**
This drawing (right), from Gingoire's *Castel of Laboures*,
shows a man sitting on a low settle at a trestle table,
and on the wall by the window there is a bracket with a
hand towel, bowl and, above it, a reservoir of clean water.
As fingers were used rather than forks, washing was
important and the facilities are shown in many drawings.

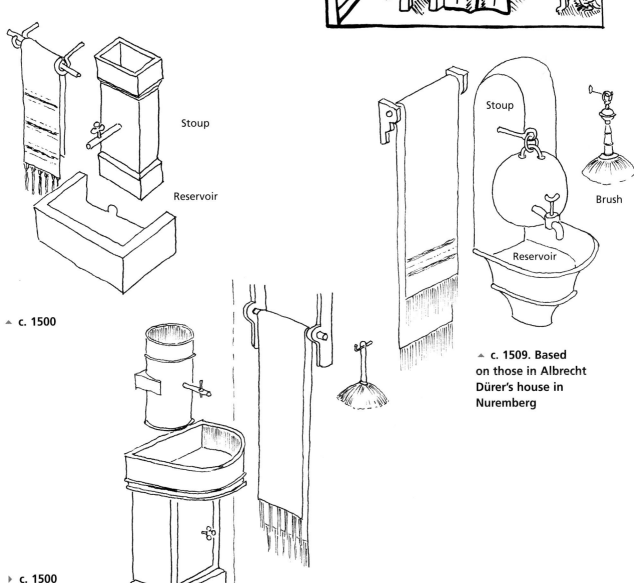

Stoup

Reservoir

▲ **c. 1500**

▶ **c. 1500**

Stoup

Brush

Reservoir

▲ **c. 1509. Based
on those in Albrecht
Dürer's house in
Nuremberg**

BATHS

A fifteenth-century document describes a bathtub made for Henry VII thus:

'Having sheets round about ye roof, do thus as ye mean every sheet full of flowers and herbs soote and green and look you have sponges 5 or 6 thereon to sit or lean look there be a great sponge thereon your soverign to sit thereon a sheet and so he may bathe hym there to fit.'

Henry VIII inherited a number of tubs, and left tiled sunken baths, with hot and cold running water.

It is difficult to prove how often he used them, but we know that on medical grounds he had at least one medicinal herb bath each winter; we also know that he avoided baths when 'the sweating sickness' was prevalent. Perhaps it is this avoidance that gave rise to the belief that bathing was a dangerous activity.

Baths, when used in a domestic situation, tended to be simple wooden tubs set up in front of a fire, with water being brought in buckets from the kitchens. Lots of buckets would be required as it would take at least 30 gallons (approximately 136 litres) to fill a bathtub.

PROJECT
MAKE A BATH

1 Take a piece of stout cardboard tube with a minimum diameter of 3in (7.5cm) and about 2½in (6.5cm) high. Cover the inner and outer surfaces of the tube with self-adhesive wooden flooring.

2 When all is set, fit a round base in the tube and finally bind it with twine to resemble rope, as shown on the right in the photograph below.

An inventory from Whitehall Palace, London, taken in 1543 lists in the bathroom: '*35 towels of Holland linen, A selection of bathrobes, Curtains, Coffins, Pailes, Stomachers and Sloppes*'. The last four items being various kinds of cloth used.

Collapsible beds – known as trussing beds because they spent so much time trussed up – are often listed as part of the bathroom furniture, too, and inside the bath it was not unusual to have a bench, stool or form, which stood on deal floorboards.

Most illustrations of the period have baths, beds and banquets hand-in-hand with mixed bathing, music and a jolly old time. But we won't go into that side of life here. Suffice to say there were more baths in such establishments than anywhere else.

Some people did use water to clean themselves, and once again period prints show small reservoirs with a tap (see page 93). These are mounted or hung above a basin or stoup and at hand are a small brush and a towel. There are so many shapes there must be one that would fit into your dolls' house.

BATHS IN RELATION TO HYGIENE

Bathing had nothing to do with physical cleanliness. It was more a ritual of religion, chivalry or magic, and 'ablutions' were to remove the invisible stains of death, madness or disease, even the touching of people of an inferior sort. Murderers or women after childbirth warranted a bath, but not to remove dirt. Ritual was taken to extreme when Pontius Pilate took water and washed his hands saying, 'I am innocent of the blood of this just person'.

Knight of the Bath was indeed a knight of the bathtub. In 1399 Henry IV instituted a ritual initiation which put the candidate in the care of two '*esquires of honour grave well seen in courtship and nurture and also in feats of chivalry*'. They saw to it that he was shaved, had a hair cut and a bath. The bathtub was hung inside and out with rich cloth but no mention is made of hot water. Two ancient knights then instructed him in ways of chivalry before pouring more water over him. He was then put in a bed without hangings where he stayed until dry, then he was dressed and taken to the chapel where, with the priest, chandler and watch, he kept vigil until sunrise, when he became a Knight of the Bath and could hold the King's towel.

At Leeds Castle in Kent there is a reconstruction of a room known as the Queen's Bathroom. The queen in question was Queen Catherine de Valois, but the room is an Edwardian idea of what luxurious surroundings royal ladies may have enjoyed, and that is just what most of us do with our dolls' houses. Catherine was only 21 years old when her husband, King Henry V died. She, after a while, fell in love with and secretly married the Clerk of her Wardrobe, Owen Tudor. Their son, Edmund was the father of Henry VII, the first of the Tudor kings.

The bath, like most, is surprisingly simple but is hung with fine white curtains suspended from a sparver canopy, a sign of rank. This is round, the same size as the bath, with a conical cap or cover. The lower edge could be decorated in one of many ways, but the best looked like a coronet. It was from the inside of this canopy that the side drapes or curtains were hung.

There are various types of bucket to fill the bath, which in turn was emptied through a tap towards the bottom. The fireplace in the room has a semicircular hood complementing the canopy of the bath, all part of the Edwardian dream.

CHAPTER FIVE
HEATING

The 'Nook' • Domestic Fireplaces • To Cap It All: Chimneys

THE 'NOOK'

A 'nook' was that special place in which the fire was set, but later it became a corner in that same place, and even the cheek or jamb supporting the chimney breast. Before the introduction of fire baskets and the use of coal there wasn't even room to consider sitting there. Much later than our period the Edwardians were the romantics who created inglenooks – a bench or seat built beside the fireplace – introducing the myth into our culture.

In the Tudor/Stewart period, fireplaces were wide to accommodate long logs, which reduced the labour required to harvest them. Young boys were employed to crouch in this corner, protected by a special shield, while they turned the spit, making sure your dinner was 'done to a turn'. So who would want to relax in such a place in the certain knowledge that it would be they who were 'done'?

The man or small boy who turned the spit could not leave his post, and so risk burning the meat in his care and the wrath of his master if he did so. As a result, he became so hot and uncomfortable that, to overcome the dehydration and thirst, he drank great amounts of ale. Now understand that what goes in must come out, resulting in some rather unsavoury habits. The names applied to him and his trade were 'Jacke who turneth the broche', 'turnbroach' or 'turnspit', and until the late seventeenth century when they were replaced by cheaper and more convenient mechanical devices such as spit jacks, their names were terms of contempt solely, due to their foul habits.

In some large fireplaces the cob irons that carried the spits full of meat were mounted on sloping brick walls, which gave them support, concentrating the heat of the fire forward but also giving some shelter to the 'turnspit'.

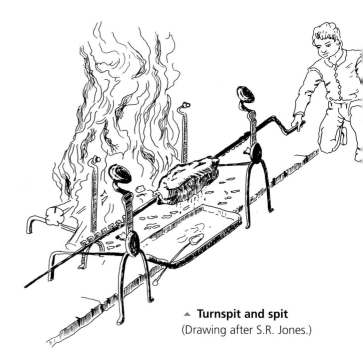

▲ **Turnspit and spit**
(Drawing after S.R. Jones.)

▲ **'Jacke who turneth the broche'**
This detail, after an Italian woodcut of c. 1570, shows Jacke hiding behind a tall, rectangular screen. Refined versions of these screens, made of richer materials, were brought into the parlour or other living areas to protect the delicate complexion of the lady of the house.

Elizabethan/Jacobean Pole Screen

This screen is based on one at Plas Mawr, Conwy, north Wales, a merchant's house of c. 1577. While the original screen is made of basketwork, I used garden twine to represent straw for my model, which I coiled, gluing it as I went, to give the correct size. This is held in place by a metal pin which can be given a handle, or you could use a simple wooden dowel.

The supporting pole is made up of two long pieces of wood with matching holes in them to support the circular screen at the desired height. These supporting poles are kept the required distance apart by small strips of wood or spacers glued top and bottom. They must be of sufficient thickness to allow the screen to move as and when required. The finial at the top of the posts can be carved, cast or simply cut from a suitable newel post or suchlike. The base or stand is made in the form of a cross and can have simple feet and brackets to support the pole. Over the years these became much more refined.

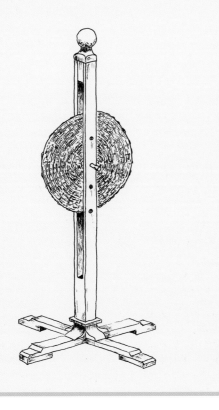

Kitchen Fire Screen

To protect themselves from the fierce heat of the kitchen fire, there were various devices. The straw target, which was used in the compulsory archery practice was brought indoors and mounted on a special stand of metal or wood so that it could be positioned between the 'turn-broche' and the fire. If not kept wet, it could catch fire, so the one below is in a lead-lined box which would contain water, to prevent it going up in flames. Others had a metal stand, while some were mounted in a simple frame and kept damp with water from a jug or bucket.

CLOCKWORK SPIT JACKS

In the village of Berkeley, Gloucestershire, there is a memorial to one Thomas Peirce who died aged 77 in 1665. It reads as follows:

Here Lyeth Thomas Peirce, whom no man taught
Yet he in Iron, Brasse, and Silver wrought
He Jacks, and Clocks, and watches (with Art) made
And mended too when others worke did fade
Of Berkeley five tymes Mayor this Artist was
And yet this Mayor, this Artist was but Grasse
When his own watch was downe on the last Day
He that made watches had not made A Key
To winde it Up, but Useless it must lie
Untill he Rise Again no more to Die

▲ **A model clockwork spit jack**

▲ **A smoke jack being used**
(Drawing after a period woodcut.)

Thomas Peirce was a young apprentice aged 15 years when Elizabeth I died, and made spit jacks, clocks and watches until he died, a man of some standing in the town of his birth.

Clockwork spit jacks had been made since at least 1587 and were driven by large stones of some 14lb (6.35kg) in weight. These jacks, like the clocks of the period, were mechanically simple but in the hands of a craftsman could be quite ornate. Originals were still being used and new ones made in the mid-nineteenth century.

SMOKE JACKS

The smoke jack harnessed the flow of hot air from great kitchen fires as it rushed up the chimney. There are numerous such devices shown in period illustrations from mainland Europe, but it is thought that this device came late to Britain and was not widely used until c. 1720.

There was a house fire in the city of Norwich in 1507 and, when the site was excavated in 1971–8, an iron shaft was discovered in the debris which had been used as the vertical shaft of a smoke jack similar to that shown top right. Another better-preserved and better-known example is to be found in the Tudor kitchen at Cowdray House, Midhurst, West Sussex, but the exact date of its insertion is not known. What is certain is that smoke jacks were not suitable for insertion in the vast chimneys of most Tudor houses. Tudor chimneys were wide but, to encourage a draught strong enough to turn a spit, required a narrow flue, one brought down to around 24in (61cm) in diameter, and there are many illustrations of these from the fifteenth century on.

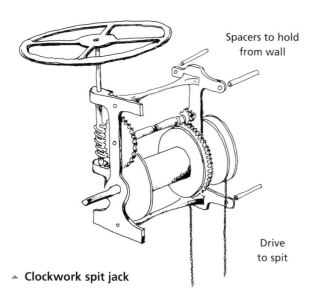

Spacers to hold from wall

Drive to spit

▲ **Clockwork spit jack**

THE DOG-WHEEL

In a kitchen in 1536 Dr Caius made notes for his book *Of Englishe Dogges* and wrote:

A certain dog in kitchen service excellent. For when any meat is to be roasted they go into a wheel, they turning about with the weight of their bodies so diligently look to their business that no drudge or scullion can do the feat more cunningly.

The dogs in question were much like the present-day Jack Russell, but with longer bodies, and they were trained to run in a small treadmill. The mill consisted of a wheel 36in (91.4cm) in diameter and 12in (30.5cm) wide, mounted by an iron axle to the wall next to and above the fireplace. To to be accurate, the dog wheel should only be used in dolls' houses from South Wales and south-west England.

SPIT DOGS AND FIRE DOGS

There are many variations of these on the market. The captions to the illustrations below describe their correct use.

Cresset cups, or the brackets for them, were incorporated in the tops of some spit dogs and there is a debate with miniaturists as to how they were used – to hold and mull wine or to hold fat for basting the meat being roasted. The answer lies in the old English word 'craisset' and French 'cresset' which is a vessel to hold grease or oil. Sorry, I quite liked the idea of mulled ale or wine, but they made that by the bucket.

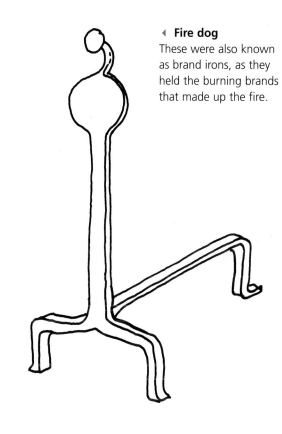

◁ **Fire dog**
These were also known as brand irons, as they held the burning brands that made up the fire.

◁ **Spit dog or 'andiron'**
These held the spits used for cooking meat, and had a series of hooks or rests to carry the spits at the required height. The basic fire dog did not have these hooks. Note the cresset cup on top.

◁ **Creeper**
These are a third type, which I have never seen in miniature, but they can be made by cutting down a pair of fire dogs. They were small and put under broken, part-burnt, logs to prevent them from creeping on to the room floor.

⏴ Cob irons

Spits used in the roasting of meat were carried on 'andirons', or the larger form, cob irons. Cob irons had feet at one end which rested on the front of the hearth. The other end rested against the back wall of the fireplace. These are at Hampton Court.

⏴ Cob irons, Plas Mawr, Conwy, North Wales

Cob irons are a type of spit dog, used in larger houses.

⏶ Cob irons rest on the brick wall at the back, and a clockwork spit jack can be seen

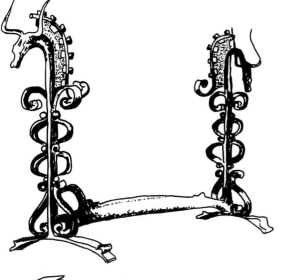

FIRE BASKETS

Fire baskets were introduced when coal became available in quantity. Unlike wood, it burned best when held in a mass and would not burn well next to the floor. There are many regional variations, but the one below is to be found in the Little Castle, Bolsover, Derbyshire. If you were burning coal, you might require spit dogs, but would not need brand irons or creepers.

▲ **Iron Age double-ended fire dogs**
One shown with the logs in position. This type can be made out of wood and painted to look like metal.

DOMESTIC FIREPLACES

The central point of focus of many rooms is the fireplace, which is just as it should be, as the term is derived from '*focus*', the Latin for 'hearth'.

In years past, smoke emanating from a house was an indicator of wealth and/or social standing and, if you could afford to produce this smoke, you could afford to pay 'Peter's Pence'. This was a hearth tax introduced originally in the tenth century to produce revenue for the Pope. The tax was finally abolished in 1534, when the crown diverted the cash for their own use. This punitive tax was instrumental in restricting the number of fireplaces in most homes to just one.

Even quality houses with a more private withdrawing area only had one, and while this area or room may have been comfortably furnished it was, in the winter at least, cold.

THE OVERCROWDED CHIMNEYPIECE

Tudor hall fireplaces are one of the most striking elements in mid-to-late Tudor houses. Bold statements were the norm, and Hans Holbein the Younger drew elevations for a fine hall fireplace for his patron Henry VIII, which was intended for his new palace at Bridewell. It is a whimsical design with Doric columns below and ionic ones above. The columns are squat in relation to their height but as other builders picked up the same basic design it established general principles now regarded as good Tudor design.

Two of the best overmantels of the period and style were re-mounted one on top of the other in the Great Hall at Burton Agnes, North Humberside in 1762. The upper one, carved in wood in 1570, was painted to look like stone. The lower section, carved in 1610, shows the story of the Wise and Foolish Virgins.

HISTORICAL REFERENCE

Portable fires – braziers, or charcoal burners – were a way of avoiding the hearth tax, and Hampton Court has at least one matching pair from c. 1600. Some braziers were mounted on runners, while others had brackets that allowed them to be moved with the aid of stout poles or handles.

A more refined version was the foot warmer. This could be made of various materials and was used in the bedroom, in carriages and even under the table. Most of these do not survive as, strangely, they were made of wood, with a metal tray or ceramic pot inside to hold the hot embers.

Early to mid-Tudor hall houses had a fire in the middle of the floor, and the smoke from these escaped through unglazed windows or via a louvre in the roof. These louvres could be most ornate, architectural features, or far more basic, like those still to be found on the ridges of many a village hall.

Many different experiments were carried out to encourage the smoke to leave the room, perhaps the most interesting being that mentioned in 1535: '*Tunnills by which the smoke of the Hearth is Wonder strange conveyed*' out of the house. These strange 'tunnills' were in the underside of the arch of a large window, as in the east end window at Clevedon Court, Somerset.

Much more simple were the decorative ridge tiles incorporating vents, placed at intervals, which allowed some of the smoke to escape. This wasn't very satisfactory, so the 'smoke bay' was introduced to convey the fumes up to the ridge. This was simply a wall, built at one end of the room and along the full width, to form a massive chimney breast. To work, the fire had to be moved from the central position it had occupied for centuries, to a position against this wall. This repositioning and the whole ingenious idea gave us the fireplace with a chimney.

PROJECT
FIREPLACE WITH CHOICE OF OVERMANTELS

There appears to have been a set width for such chimneypieces and I make all of mine 6in (15cm) wide, but the height depends on the room you plan to put it in. You can make a fireplace as deep as you wish to take your own fire dogs or basket, but remember to make the hearth project forward.

1 Cut two pieces of wood 3in (7.6cm) wide and the same height as the room in which the fireplace will be placed.

2 Mark out and cut the arch forming the fireplace. Then fix the two pieces together with strips of waste wood on the back.

3 If you wish to have spice cupboards incorporated in the overmantel, cut the holes for these now, and make and fit the small boxes – to form the inside of these cupboards – at this stage, too.

4 Cut and fit the hearth 6in (15.2cm) wide and make sure it projects forward just sufficient to take the columns you wish to fit either side.

5 Next fix the sides, which must be the height of your room and of a width/depth to take your fire irons.

6 Fit ready-made columns either side of the fire, gluing them to the hearth and the fireplace front.

7 Now assemble the mantel shelf, using mouldings of your choice. The continuous cornice at the top of the overmantel should be of the same construction. The overmantel should be the same height as the fireplace section, which is dictated by the columns used.

8 The section above the cornice can be anything from ½in (1.2cm) to 6in (15.2cm) high, depending on your room height.

9 Many chimneypieces of this period were of stone or of carved oak, while some were a mixture of stone fireplace and wood overmantel. They would have been painted and gilded, or decorated with rich inlay, so remember this when finishing off. Others were decorated by skilled plasterers first, then painted.

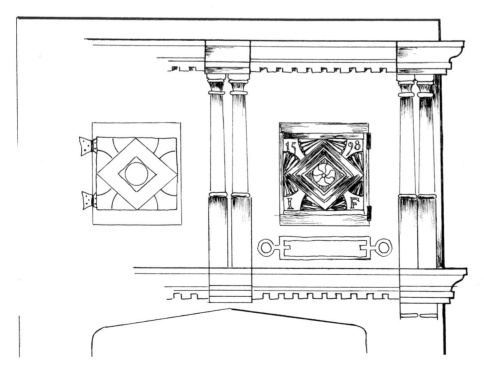

◄ **Overmantel with spice cupboards**
At first spice cupboards were small units, which hung on the wall next to the fire, but by 1550 they were built into fine overmantels, keeping the contents dry and under the eye of the head of the house. Here, two types of hinge are shown, but the exposed ones are the most simple to fit (an alternative overmantel is shown overleaf).

Nikolaus Pevsner, the architectural historian, said that the remounted overmantels in the Great Hall at Burton Agnes constituted the 'most crazily overcrowded chimney piece of all England', which just begs you to try to interpret its details.

Most overmantels were not so grand as those, but impressive just the same, being richly carved or decorated, and could incorporate the family coat of arms, scenes from mythology, lamp or candle brackets, and spice cupboards – the choice is yours.

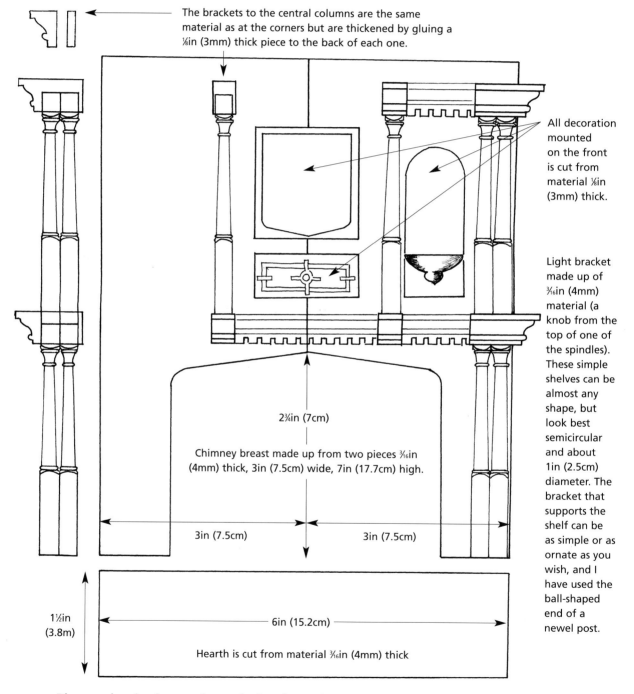

The brackets to the central columns are the same material as at the corners but are thickened by gluing a ⅛in (3mm) thick piece to the back of each one.

All decoration mounted on the front is cut from material ⅛in (3mm) thick.

Light bracket made up of 3/16in (4mm) material (a knob from the top of one of the spindles). These simple shelves can be almost any shape, but look best semicircular and about 1in (2.5cm) diameter. The bracket that supports the shelf can be as simple or as ornate as you wish, and I have used the ball-shaped end of a newel post.

2⅜in (7cm)

Chimney breast made up from two pieces 3/16in (4mm) thick, 3in (7.5cm) wide, 7in (17.7cm) high.

3in (7.5cm)

3in (7.5cm)

1½in (3.8m)

6in (15.2cm)

Hearth is cut from material 3/16in (4mm) thick

▲ **Diagram showing how coving and other decoration is mounted on the overmantel**

TO CAP IT ALL: CHIMNEYS

Even chimneys became a work of art, starting from things as simple as an old barrel fixed in the thatched ridge of a roof, and ending in the most ornate brickwork of the Tudor and Jacobean periods. This finishing off – making the top weatherproof and capping them – was important, but taken to extremes with some very decorative results.

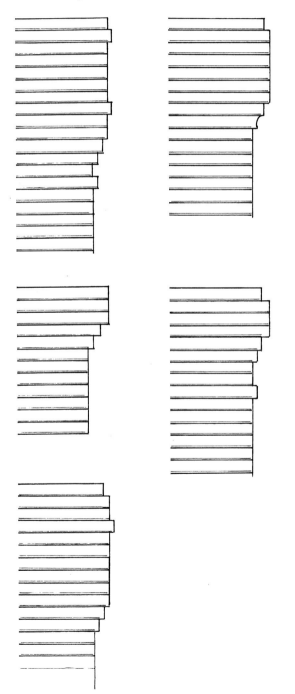

You may have heard of the famous dolls' house at Uppark, West Sussex, but not seen the chimney pots on the roof of the mansion it resides in. They are restorations following a disastrous fire but keep up an old tradition with the potter putting simple, everyday comments or quotes in the wet clay. One made in October 1991 has an inscription which simply reads 'Margaret Thatcher resigned as I was making this'. You could record events on your chimney, rooting your dolls' house in your chosen period.

CROSS SECTIONS OF CHIMNEY CAPS

There were many variations of chimney caps, but the diagrams on the left are of simple ones, dating from 1525 to 1600. They show how successive courses of brick were laid, giving a simple but decorative outline. What the drawings don't show is that while the basic chimney may be of square section, it could also be of a round or even hexagonal section. All are made of unmoulded square-ended bricks, so to make these you simply require blocks of wood the same shape as the body of the stack, but larger and of various thicknesses, depending on the number of brick courses involved.

STACK THEM HIGH

It is quite simple to make at least some of the brick chimneys so beloved by the Tudors, using basic materials such as card, wood and paper. This may sound a bit like a primary school project but the results will look very authentic.

STAR-SHAPED STACKS

These are also quite simple to make using a length of square section wood as the basic form, then fixing lengths of small triangular section wood in the centre of each face. For the best results the triangular strips should be used, with sides one-third the width of the square section used. There are many variations on this basic form, which my diagrams will help you to achieve.

PROJECT

A SPIRAL CHIMNEY WITH CONCAVE SIDES

The spiral chimney is one of the most attractive to be found on Tudor and Stewart houses and is quite simple to make using square pieces of wood glued one on top of the other as in the diagram.

To make this, mount 1in or 1¼in (25mm or 32mm) squares of wood of a thickness that would represent a brick at 1/12 scale, i.e. ³⁄₁₆ –¼in (4–6mm). Drill a small hole in the centre of each square piece of wood, and through these holes push a stout wire or a fine wooden dowel to hold them together.

Glue these squares together, with each one slightly out of line with the one beneath it, which will result in a rough spiral. Sand this back to give a smooth finish, using a piece of sandpaper stuck to a short length of broom shank or dowel up to 1in (25mm) diameter. If the finish is still not as fine as you would like it, finish it off with filler.

The cap of this pot is square, as is the base, and should be given small crenellations made by using short lengths of wood with a ¼in (6mm) square section. In plan there are two rows of these pieces of wood, one inside the other, with the outside ones being the tallest or merlon, and the lower the crenel.

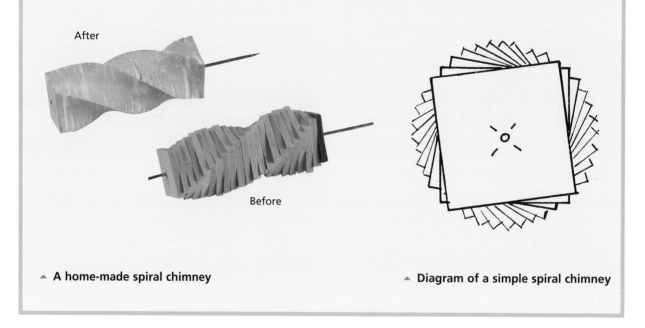

▲ **A home-made spiral chimney**

▲ **Diagram of a simple spiral chimney**

ROUND CHIMNEY STACKS

These can be cut from dowel, card or plastic tube to which you can glue all sorts of shapes, resulting in spiral or chequered effects. You can even use embossed paper or some of the shapes cut from it and mounted on your model.

HEXAGONAL SHAPES

Here the base and cap are constructed using hexagonal sections of a slightly larger size. Once again, it looks complicated to cap a hexagon but it is basically simple, using only one block of wood cut to the required shape before the top is brought back to a hexagon. The star-shaped cap should be of a height or thickness to represent 4–6 courses of thin bricks with the hexagon on top being the same section as the body of the stack, but only 2–3 courses high.

GRAPHS FOR CIRCULAR CHIMNEY STACKS

Circular chimneys can be decorated in many ways, using thin brick tiles or card cut to size, then glued in position. The graphs below show a selection of ideas. Cut a piece of graph paper the size of the chimney to be decorated, then it is quite simple to work out where to glue your card or tiles. Mark the positions on the paper then prick through this to mark the chimney.

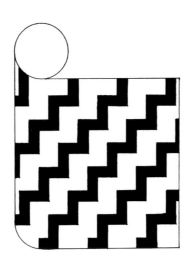
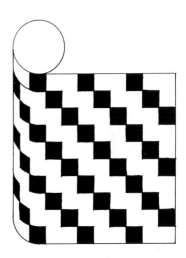

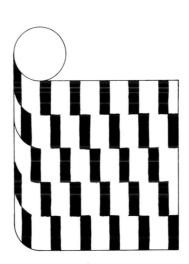
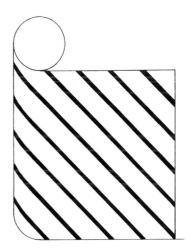

Hampton Court Palace

These chimneys are Victorian copies of Tudor originals. They look best when mounted in groups (see facing page) and even better when their caps are joined together, as here, which also makes them stronger. Sometimes even the bodies of the chimneys are joined, being built as one unit.

HISTORICAL REFERENCE

Wages were not high, and craftsmen had to subsidize their income by lending their hand to other work from time to time. They had considerable skill and showed great ingenuity in the variety of decoration, cut or moulded, applied to the brick chimneys they made.

Shropshire's finest Tudor house, Plaish Hall, was the home of Assize Judge William Leighton, who enlisted the help of the local Sheriff to find the best and most skilled chimney-maker to work on his house. He said there was only one man in the county up to the task but he had just been sentenced to death for sheep stealing, and it was the Judge himself who had sentenced him. On learning this, Judge Leighton had the wretched man removed from his cell and set to work at Plaish Hall, building the coveted chimneys. When the work was completed to the satisfaction of the Judge, the chimney carver-cum-sheep-rustler was returned to his cell and on to the place of execution where 'The Judge made his neck to crack'.

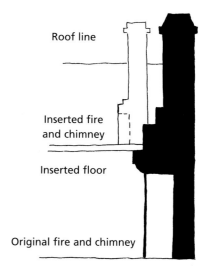

Dingestow Farmhouse, Monmouthshire

Section showing position of the inserted first-floor fire.

GROUPING

Owners were proud of these ornate chimneys and few stand in isolation. Most groups were just for show, with many fires having three ornate chimneys, so do think groups. As time passed, and more fireplaces were introduced into the home, they tended to be just where they were required with little thought of how this would affect the elevation of the house viewed by a visitor.

It was not long before it was realized that putting fireplaces in groups, back to back, above each other made the chimneys easier to build and kept the house warmer. It also made a bold statement when, with its magnificent brickwork, it finally broke through the roof into the sky for everyone to see.

▼ **Groups of chimneys**

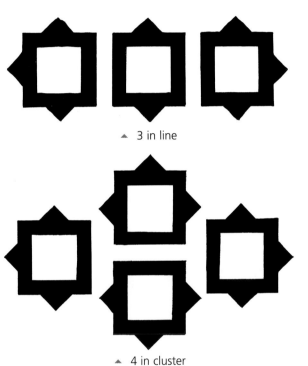

▲ 3 in line

▲ 4 in cluster

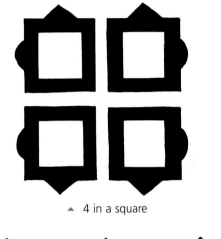

▲ 4 in a square

▲ 3 in line, with one different shape or diamondwise

DINGESTOW FARMHOUSE, MONMOUTHSHIRE, WALES

This simple hall house (right) was built c. 1525, and is quite advanced for its time, having a fireplace and chimney, not the traditional fire in the middle of the floor. It still had one large room, the hall, open to the roof but around 1625 a floor was inserted to give an upstairs room. The fireplace for this room, built into the roof space, sits on the mantel shelf of the original ground floor fireplace and the two chimneys break through the roof quite independently of each other.

CHAPTER SIX

COOKING AND FOOD

Tudor Kitchen Room Box • Ovens and Cooking Utensils
• Food Preservation and Storage • Cutlery v. Fingers • Banqueting Hall Room Box

TUDOR KITCHEN ROOM BOX

Stirling Castle has a kitchen full of period atmosphere and bustling kitchen staff, lost in the gloomy mists of steam, smoke and soot. Hampton Court Palace has much larger kitchens, which were just as busy but have a different atmosphere with fifteen or more offices, each devoted to one part of the meal. Food passed through these and the great kitchen into small rooms known as 'dressers', which were full of garnishes and sauces.

These rooms served the same purpose as a 'dressing table', a table which was also known as a 'dresser' (see right). For the model below, based on the Great Kitchens at Hampton Court, I have taken just a few of these elements and put them into one large room, encased in a brick shell. Charcoal-burning stoves for more delicate food, the great roasting fireplace and a bank of three ovens for bread, pies and pastries are but a few of the elements selected for this room. We could not hope to build it all, but I hope that this morsel, will give you a taste of period cooking.

▶ **Front view of the kitchen**
The front has been decorated to look like the diaper work of the period – when decorating your own model you can choose from the patterns shown on pages 44–5. When the kitchen is complete, the front slides up and down, held in place by two strips of wood on the inside, and the edges of the small turrets on the outside.

▲ **Dressers**

These were originally tables on which you dressed food or clothes. These enormous chests are quite late and, when you lift the lid, there is a tray for cutlery.

▲ **Kitchen table**

A table displaying food from the period.

▲ **The kitchen**

Details shown in the photographs can be installed as required, and it can be great fun making or collecting these.

PROJECT

A TUDOR KITCHEN ROOM BOX

The outer shell of the kitchen is a three-sided box – you could use MDF, foamboard or plywood. Within this is a second box, which has the openings to the various cooking stations which are housed in a 2in (5cm) deep cavity between the outer an inner box. These cooking stations have to be assembled as in the drawings. They must be at least part-decorated before they are fitted permanently in position, then placed against the inner face of an outer wall, before the inner box with the relevant openings is placed in front of it.

Start with the left-hand side wall and the bread ovens, then the back walls with the great roasting range and finally, the right-hand wall with the charcoal burners.

The tops of the resulting cavity walls have to be capped with flat pieces of wood, and small blocks of wood or other material are needed on their underside to hold them in place. If you wish to light the various ranges from above or behind, do not glue these down, as you may wish to remove them from time to time to change light bulbs, and so on.

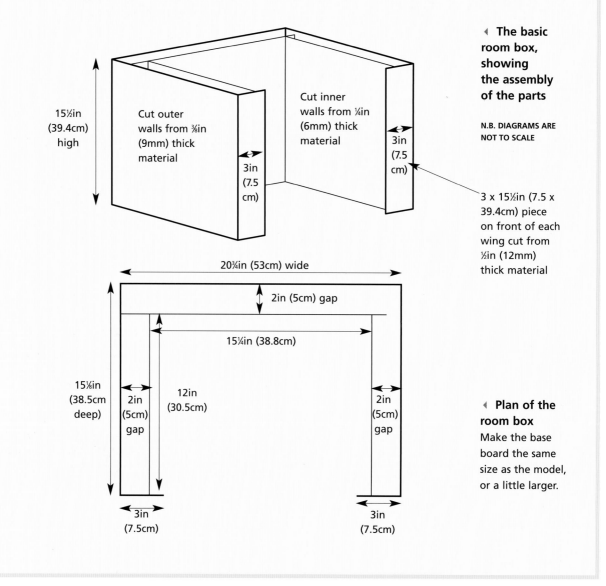

◄ **The basic room box, showing the assembly of the parts**

N.B. DIAGRAMS ARE NOT TO SCALE

15½in (39.4cm) high

Cut outer walls from ⅜in (9mm) thick material

3in (7.5 cm)

Cut inner walls from ¼in (6mm) thick material

3in (7.5 cm)

3 x 15½in (7.5 x 39.4cm) piece on front of each wing cut from ½in (12mm) thick material

20¾in (53cm) wide

2in (5cm) gap

15¼in (38.8cm)

15⅛in (38.5cm deep)

2in (5cm) gap

12in (30.5cm)

2in (5cm) gap

3in (7.5cm)

3in (7.5cm)

◄ **Plan of the room box**
Make the base board the same size as the model, or a little larger.

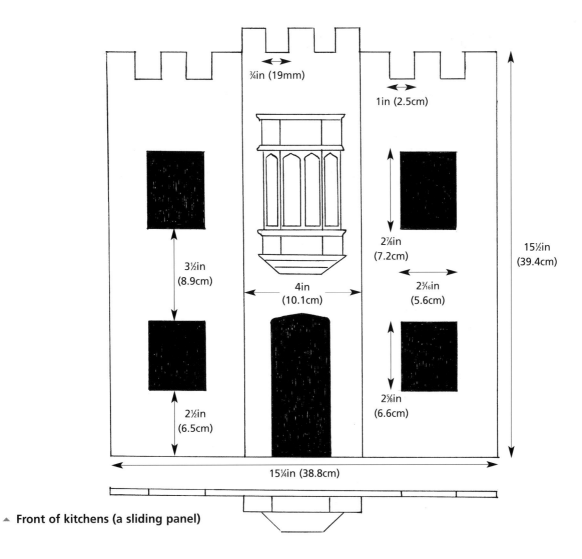

¾in (19mm)

1in (2.5cm)

15½in (39.4cm)

2⅞in (7.2cm)

2³⁄₁₆in (5.6cm)

3½in (8.9cm)

4in (10.1cm)

2⅝in (6.6cm)

2½in (6.5cm)

15¼in (38.8cm)

▲ **Front of kitchens (a sliding panel)**

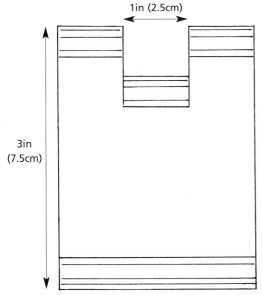

1in (2.5cm)

3in (7.5cm)

▲ **Front elevation of the side turrets – two required**
Material ½in (12mm) thick, bought moulding ⅜in (9mm)

¾in (19mm)

½in (12mm)

▲ **Side elevation**

The tops of the front walls are crenellated with stone caps to the brickwork. These caps should be cut from a large length of suitable cornice and mounted so that they project forward from the front face of the wall.

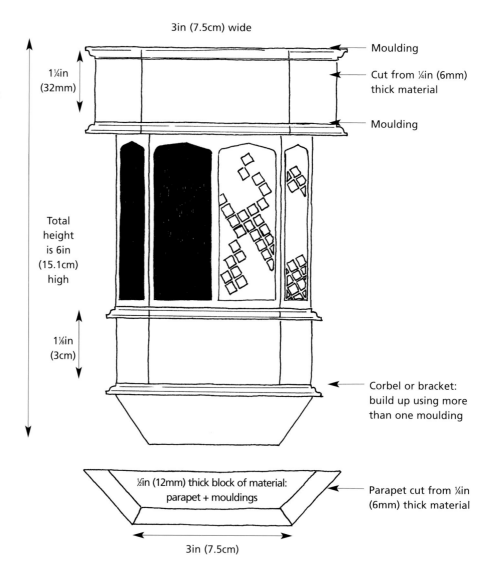

▶ Oriel window

The oriel window (right) is cut from ½in (12mm) thick material, and is 3in wide x 6in high (7.5 x 15.2cm). It is solid and just painted to look the part.

3in (7.5cm) wide

1¼in (32mm)

Total height is 6in (15.1cm) high

1⅛in (3cm)

Moulding

Cut from ¼in (6mm) thick material

Moulding

Corbel or bracket: build up using more than one moulding

½in (12mm) thick block of material: parapet + mouldings

Parapet cut from ¼in (6mm) thick material

3in (7.5cm)

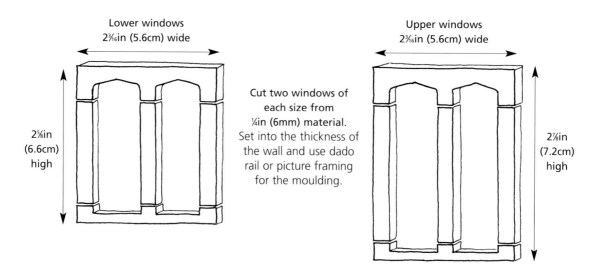

Lower windows
2³⁄₁₆in (5.6cm) wide

2⅝in (6.6cm) high

Cut two windows of each size from ¼in (6mm) material. Set into the thickness of the wall and use dado rail or picture framing for the moulding.

Upper windows
2³⁄₁₆in (5.6cm) wide

2⅞in (7.2cm) high

▲ **Upper and lower windows – of two sizes but the same basic design (not to scale)**

THE ROOF

▲ **General view of the roof timbers, showing how they are assembled**
The roof over the main room is carried on stout timbers as in the drawings overleaf. The flat tops and the wall tops are painted to look like lead, but do not fix, as you may wish to remove them to change light bulbs and so on.

THE ROOF

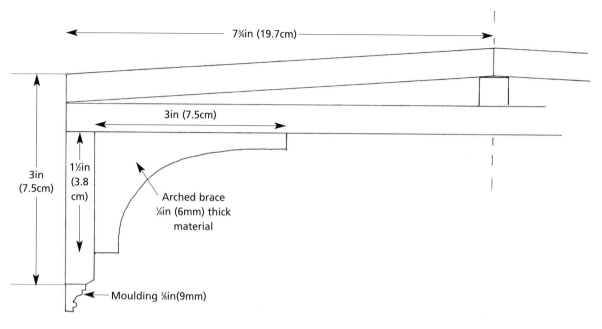

7¾in (19.7cm)

3in (7.5cm)

3in (7.5cm)

1½in (3.8 cm)

Arched brace ¼in (6mm) thick material

Moulding ⅜in(9mm)

▲ **Roof timbers**
Cut from ½in (12mm) square material

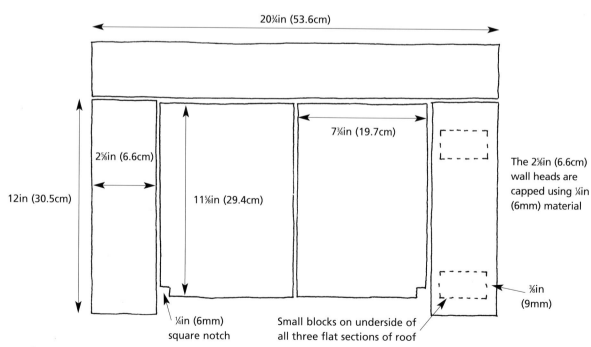

20¾in (53.6cm)

7¾in (19.7cm)

2⅝in (6.6cm)

12in (30.5cm)

11⅝in (29.4cm)

The 2⅝in (6.6cm) wall heads are capped using ¼in (6mm) material

¼in (6mm) square notch

Small blocks on underside of all three flat sections of roof

⅜in (9mm)

▲ **Roof details**

LEFT-HAND WALL

◀ **Bread ovens**
Cob irons are resting under the inglenook fireplace, back wall.

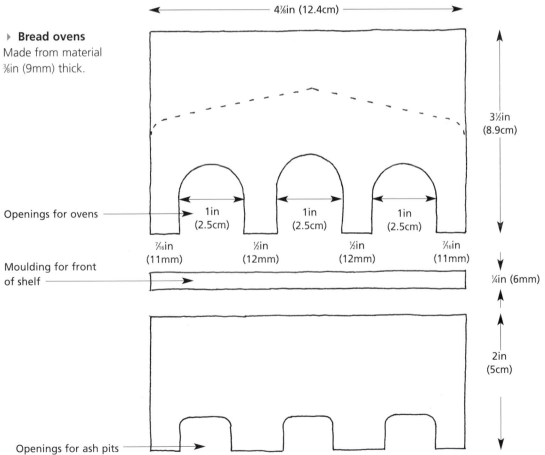

▶ **Bread ovens**
Made from material ⅜in (9mm) thick.

4⅞in (12.4cm)

3½in (8.9cm)

Openings for ovens

1in (2.5cm)   1in (2.5cm)   1in (2.5cm)

⁷⁄₁₆in (11mm)   ½in (12mm)   ½in (12mm)   ⁷⁄₁₆in (11mm)

Moulding for front of shelf

¼in (6mm)

2in (5cm)

Openings for ash pits

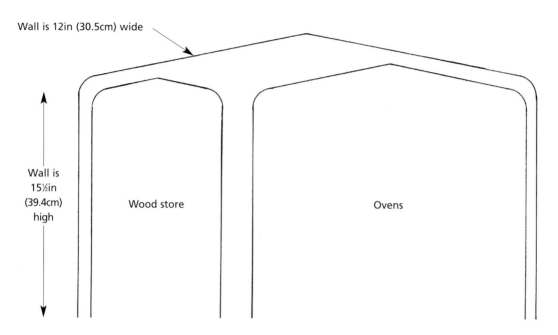

Wall is 12in (30.5cm) wide

Wall is 15½in (39.4cm) high

Wood store

Ovens

▲ **Left-hand wall, showing the edge of the wood, and the woodstore and ovens cut into it**

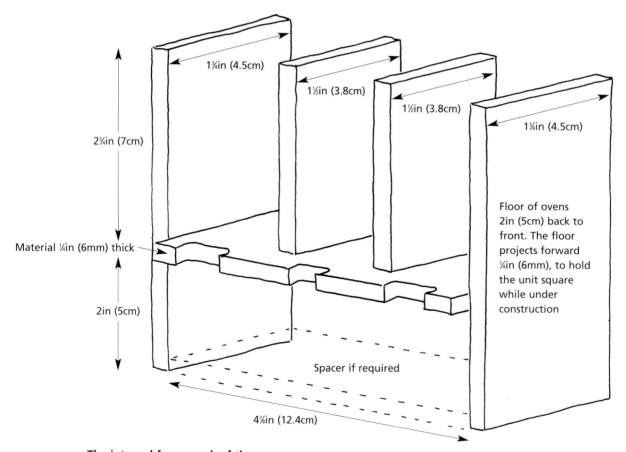

2¾in (7cm)

1¾in (4.5cm)

1½in (3.8cm)

1½in (3.8cm)

1¾in (4.5cm)

Material ¼in (6mm) thick

2in (5cm)

Floor of ovens 2in (5cm) back to front. The floor projects forward ¼in (6mm), to hold the unit square while under construction

Spacer if required

4⅞in (12.4cm)

▲ **The internal framework of the ovens**
The notches allow the ashes from the oven to fall into the ashpit rather than the floor.

BACK WALL

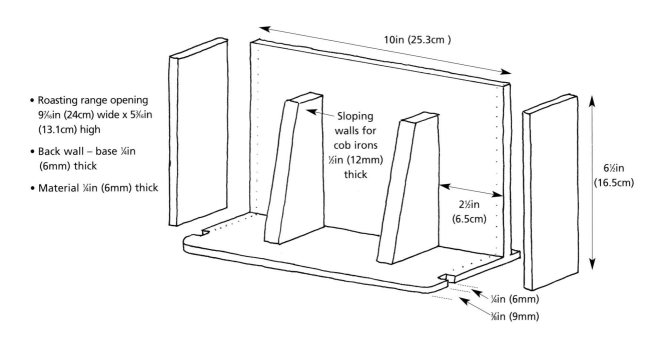

- Roasting range opening 9⁷⁄₁₆in (24cm) wide x 5³⁄₁₆in (13.1cm) high

- Back wall – base ¼in (6mm) thick

- Material ¼in (6mm) thick

10in (25.3cm)

Sloping walls for cob irons ½in (12mm) thick

6½in (16.5cm)

2½in (6.5cm)

¼in (6mm)

³⁄₈in (9mm)

▲ **Construction of large roasting range (back wall), with false wall at back to allow for electrification**

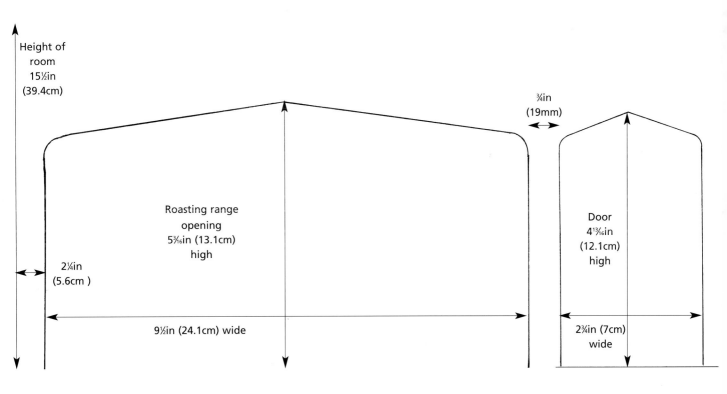

Height of room 15½in (39.4cm)

Roasting range opening 5³⁄₁₆in (13.1cm) high

2¼in (5.6cm)

9½in (24.1cm) wide

¾in (19mm)

Door 4¹³⁄₁₆in (12.1cm) high

2¾in (7cm) wide

▲ **Back wall, showing position of roasting range and door**

RIGHT-HAND WALL

▸ **Charcoal burners**

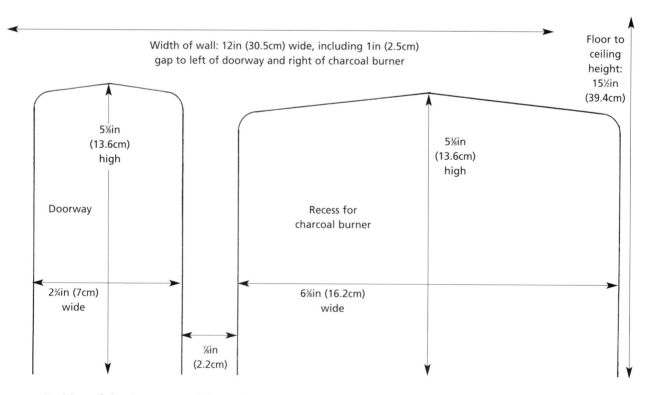

Width of wall: 12in (30.5cm) wide, including 1in (2.5cm)
gap to left of doorway and right of charcoal burner

Floor to
ceiling
height:
15½in
(39.4cm)

5⅜in
(13.6cm)
high

Doorway

2¾in (7cm)
wide

5⅜in
(13.6cm)
high

Recess for
charcoal burner

6⅜in (16.2cm)
wide

⅞in
(2.2cm)

▴ **Position of the doorway and charcoal burners on the right-hand wall**

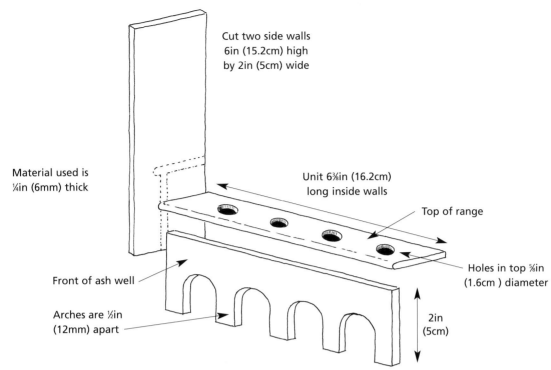

Cut two side walls
6in (15.2cm) high
by 2in (5cm) wide

Material used is
¼in (6mm) thick

Unit 6⅜in (16.2cm)
long inside walls

Top of range

Holes in top ⅝in
(1.6cm) diameter

Front of ash well

2in
(5cm)

Arches are ½in
(12mm) apart

▶ **How the charcoal burners are constructed**

▼ **A bread oven with a wooden door**

Iron doors were still a good 100 years off, so stout oak was used, as shown here. Round the edge of the door can be seen a fine line of clay used to seal it and hold it in place. The soot mark is only above the oven door, as that is where the fire was. The arch below is to the ash-pit, not a fire or heat source.

LIGHTING

If you would like light in your model, I recommend one in the fire of the large roasting range, another (orange) above the bread ovens and the same above the charcoal burners. The body of the model should have one spotlight mounted behind the roof timbers on the left-hand side. However, bear in mind that the kitchen – as well as the rest of the house – had rather poor lighting during the period, as they had to rely on candles and natural light. Strong shadows will help with the period look, so do not try to flood the room with too much light.

OVENS AND COOKING UTENSILS

In Tudor times, meat was traditionally boiled or roasted in front of a large open fire and there was no such thing as a large meat tray in a hot oven – ovens were where people made pies, cakes and bread.

There are lots of old ovens in existence and by and large they fall into two groups. First there is the bank, or group, of ovens found in the kitchens of great houses, then there is the one-off, single oven, more often than not an afterthought, built into the side of an existing fireplace. Some of these ovens projected beyond the walls of the house and had to have a roof built over them, which can be quite a feature of a dolls' house. I have seen examples of this type of oven dating from Tudor to late Georgian times and from many parts of the world, including colonial America.

In some areas the bread was traditionally put on a cabbage or other large leaf. A wooden door, not an iron one, was put in place and sealed, using clay kept close by in a bucket. A legend says the door was sealed using dough, and when the dough was cooked you knew the bread inside was ready.

▲ An outside oven of brick and stone under a stone tile roof. Surrey, England, c. 1750

This is a nice idea, but when dough on the outside was cooked the dough on the inside was overcooked.

In front of the ovens was a ledge with a narrow hole the width of the oven door in its surface. This was to allow the ashes being raked out to fall into a pit with an arched entrance beneath. This arch is often confused with a fire hole but fires beneath ovens would require flues and were still well over a 100 years away. Single, cottage-type ovens did not have this ash-pit and the baker just raked the ashes out on to the hearth.

THE SINGLE OVEN

Mostly built of brick, these were at least 36in(1m) in diameter internally and domed or beehive-shaped. In the Channel Islands such ovens are still used once a year for a special feast and are known as furze ovens in recognition of how they were heated. There was no heat source underneath but furze – or gorse – was put into the oven, topped up with thorn faggots and set on fire, then the door was closed and the interior allowed to heat up. When the required temperature was reached – having been tested by sprinkling flour to see how quickly it browned – the ashes were raked out, the bottom of the oven brushed using a mop known as a mawkin, and the pies or bread put in.

My model based on ovens at Hampton Court (see pages 110–21) has a bank of three ovens and a wood store under one large arch. There is another nice group in the basement kitchen at Bolsover Castle, Derbyshire, and a reconstruction of a more basic one at Stirling Castle, Scotland.

If you build an oven, remember it should have a wooden door, not hinged but detached, a bucket of clay to seal the door, a rake to rake out the ashes, a mawkin to mop the floor of the oven and a peel to put in and take out the bread, and so on. As a rule peels were of wood, but you may come across mention of a shod peel which was one with a metal sheath over the end of the blade. Sometimes there is a bucket of water to dampen the mawkin and bundles of twigs for fuel (see page 124). Illustrations of the period show these on the floor, under the oven or held in hooks above the oven door.

A BAKER'S EQUIPMENT

Other equipment a baker would have had included simple scales, a brush to egg the bread and so forth, and a dough box. Richer households would have a spice purse which was an ornately turned length of wood with small leather pouches full of spices attached. Lastly, a mortar mill, a wooden vessel with a rough metal rim internally, and a neat-fitting plug with a metal grater, as in my drawing overleaf.

Simple people did not run to such fine cooking machines but used much more basic methods.

▲ **Sixteenth-century house with later detached oven and chimney, Worcestershire, England**

A bake-stone was a large flat stone that was heated by placing it over red-hot embers then the dough was placed on top and baked. As early as 1600 'iron bake-stones' are mentioned in wills, marking the start in the development of the humble griddle or girdle. If you were a little better organized, then you had the bake-stone built into the back wall of the fireplace, but a little to one side.

◀ **Bread being made in the kitchen of Stirling Castle, Scotland**
Note the baker's long-handed peel.

SOME KITCHEN UTENSILS

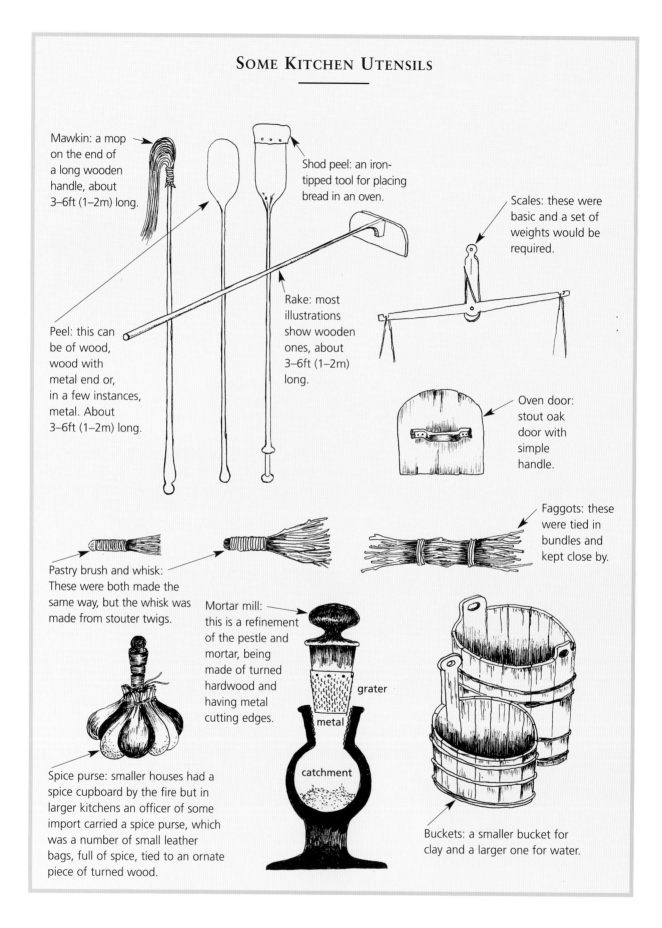

Mawkin: a mop on the end of a long wooden handle, about 3–6ft (1–2m) long.

Shod peel: an iron-tipped tool for placing bread in an oven.

Peel: this can be of wood, wood with metal end or, in a few instances, metal. About 3–6ft (1–2m) long.

Rake: most illustrations show wooden ones, about 3–6ft (1–2m) long.

Scales: these were basic and a set of weights would be required.

Oven door: stout oak door with simple handle.

Faggots: these were tied in bundles and kept close by.

Pastry brush and whisk: These were both made the same way, but the whisk was made from stouter twigs.

Mortar mill: this is a refinement of the pestle and mortar, being made of turned hardwood and having metal cutting edges.

grater

metal

catchment

Spice purse: smaller houses had a spice cupboard by the fire but in larger kitchens an officer of some import carried a spice purse, which was a number of small leather bags, full of spice, tied to an ornate piece of turned wood.

Buckets: a smaller bucket for clay and a larger one for water.

A far superior tool was the cloam oven, introduced some time prior to 1600 and still being manufactured in 1937. There are records of these being shipped out to the settlers in America. These ovens were simple, roughly made terracotta units, including the door, which was often broken and replaced by a wooden one. Ovens of this type could be built in, as at the Old Post Office, Tintagel, Cornwall, but the idea was to push them into the hot embers, heaping more around them, to heat them up.

If you couldn't afford such an oven, an upturned cauldron would do the same thing. There was also another cauldron-like variation which had a depressed lid into which hot embers were put, so the contents were cooked by heat from both above and below. Using this equipment most of the nation made bread of many regional variations.

▼ **Bronze cauldron hanging in a Tudor house**

FOOD PRESERVATION AND STORAGE

Most of us have developed a taste for smoked food and even food smoked using a particular type of wood, but smoking meat was a necessity many, many years ago.

Meat was laid in a mixture of salt and honey for seven days. It then had saltpetre rubbed into it and was left for a further two weeks before it was hung in a smoke bay or chimney. This cured the meat but it was also the only place that the flies could not live. Only when cured was the meat hung in a dry place, be it from the kitchen ceiling, or in a special ham cupboard, like that on view at Anne Hathaway's cottage. This special cupboard – which has an ornate grill for a door, to keep the cat and dog at bay – is in the left-hand side wall of the large parlour or hall fireplace. This left-hand position was traditional, and has been with us since the Stone Age for the accoutrements of the lady of the house, while his bits were on the right, right down to his and her chairs.

Fresh fish was transported in barrels of seaweed, and other fish were smoked, salted or dried. In fact much food – from sage and cherries to nuts – was simply dried. Ice was collected from frozen lakes and ponds, and used in underground stores to help the preservation of food. A 'poison pantry' held the home-made remedies that had to be made in season and these, along with more palatable preserves, were stored in jars. Depending on the contents, these jars were topped with cloth, leather, wooden bungs and butter or lard. A set of earthenware jars topped in these various ways makes a good visual display on any shelf.

Game stores held food for a short time only, and you knew by that certain odour when that time was up. Game birds, larks, rabbits, deer and eels were all hung in the same place, and these are the subject of many a period painting.

Puddings included sausages and haggis, all made from offal, so that a period pantry looked a bit like a modern delicatessen, with long, short, thin, fat and many-coloured puddings hanging there. Even some cheeses were hung, but most forms of cheese are still used today, so you don't have to look far for inspiration.

BREAD CARS

Flour was stored in a meal bin or ark, the lid of which doubled as a dough trough when making bread. If bread was required to go with the smoked ham, it was usually to be found in a bread car which hung from the ceiling, to keep it out of reach of vermin and little boys.

Bread cars were used in two ways: suspended in a fixed position over the kitchen table and, as well as the bread inside, would have herbs, onions, sausages and some small kitchen utensils hanging on the outside, all at head height, so that the cook could reach them when required; or hung via a pulley, so that it could be raised for security and lowered when required.

There were several types of bread car, but most were cage-like, being as large as a double bed or as small as a large shopping basket. Another type, which was suspended just like the others, looked like a medium-tall cupboard.

In low-ceilinged cottages, however, another technique was used: lathes were nailed across the underside of low beams to form a shelf where bread could be stored. To make these shelves more secure 'gates', or small doors, were mounted at either end, making a simple unit to build into a beamed cottage.

LIVERY, DOLE CUPBOARDS AND AUMBRY

The remains of the main meal of the day for most of the period were stored in a livery cupboard, which was a ventilated unit. With some the ventilation was via perforations cut or drilled to form patterns, but most had doors and other panels filled with rows of slats or spindles. The food was for the use of the family, and inventories record the cupboard as being in the bedroom. During the winter months much time was spent in bed, and a snack would have given comfort to a hungry child. The same cupboard, hung at the back door with food intended for the poor, was known as a dole cupboard, and some were placed in churches and even in the local jail.

An aumbry was used in various ways by the different social groups. It is thought that it took its name from the aumerer or almoner, the officer in charge of distributing 'broken meats' or leftovers to the poor. These broken meats were placed in a cupboard hung in different locations. The cupboard took on different names because its contents were for different groups of people.

The early sixteenth-century aumbry tended to be carved using outdated Gothic detail to traceried openings. To keep the flies at bay these openings had red hair cloth or wool cloth nailed inside, making them quite distinctive. The use of hair cloth spread to dole cupboards and livery cupboards as well, but most show no signs of the nails used to keep the cloth in place. This can give a miniature extra vibrancy, making it a colourful feature in a room.

▲ Bread car

▲ Livery, with bread inside – the central panel opens

PROJECT
LIVERY OR DOLE CUPBOARD

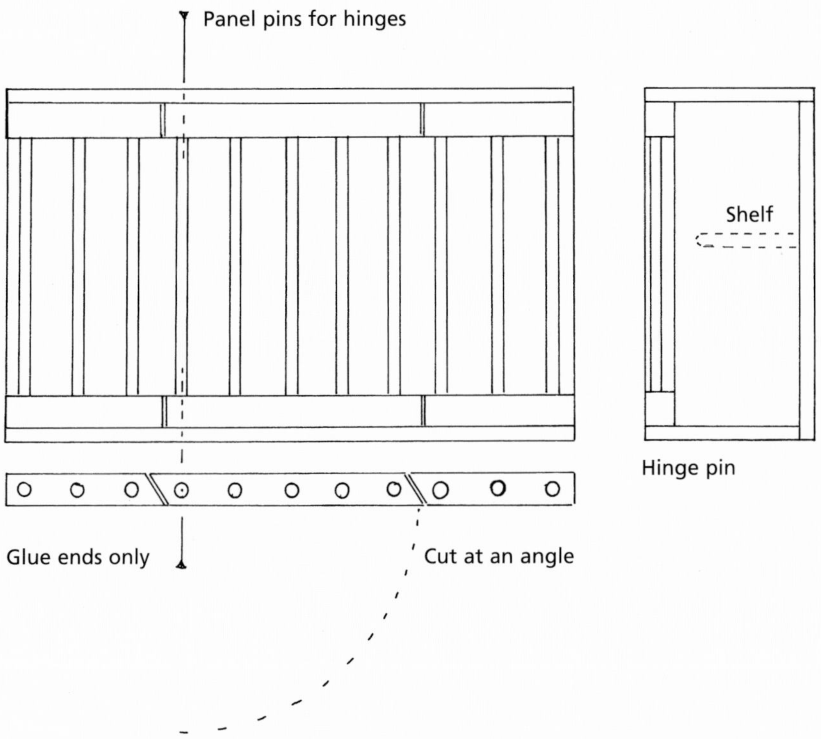

Panel pins for hinges

Shelf

Hinge pin

Glue ends only

Cut at an angle

The body of this cupboard is a simple box with a shelf inside. The front is made up of two lengths of square section and suitable spindles. When built, glue it in place but make sure you only glue above and below the end three spindles at each end. Drill small holes for panel pins to form the hinges, and cut through the frame at an angle as shown, to ensure a perfect fit for the door. No handle is required.

▶ **Livery cupboard door**
This front panel hangs in Coughton Court, Warwickshire, but, with evidence of two stout locks, it seems that it was more a serving hatch for dole distributed by the nuns of Denby Abbey. It also tends to show that such units could have been 'built in'.

**An early sixteenth-century aumbry
(also known as a 'boarded press')**
This drawing is a reconstruction of an aumbry found in
the ruins of Ivychurch Priory, Alderbury, Wiltshire.

SPICE CUPBOARDS

Spice cupboards for the most part were small units
either hung to the left of the fireplace or built into
the thickness of the wall in the same area. There
were two main shapes, one being rectangular with
bold decoration and the other almost horseshoe-
shaped in elevation.

Large houses had much larger units and at
Little Moreton Hall, Congleton, Cheshire, there
still exists a large cupboard which is long and low,
with 'drawing boxes' or drawers which were
unusual throughout the sixteenth century.

Spice cupboard at Little Moreton Hall

CUTLERY V. FINGERS

Fast food has been with us for a long time, and the
British fish and chips purchased from a fast-food
outlet has to be eaten with the fingers. That is as it
has been for centuries: if it was easier to use your
fingers, you did just that. The accepted trilogy of
knife, fork and spoon is a comparatively recent
development and the humble fork, which has been
with us for many centuries, had to fight to be
accepted on the table.

KNIVES

Knives used for eating had long and thin blades,
ground to a fine point, making a virtual single-tined
fork – ideal for spearing and holding meat. Most
old bowls and plates are rough and criss-crossed
with grooves made by these. Even the plates of
the gentry, which come down to us as precious
antiques with a smooth surface, were attacked in
this way, but had a shield to protect them. The
shield was in the form of a round wooden trencher,
set in the base of the plate, be it pewter or silver.
This gave way to the distinctive cross section of a
plate with a slight but marked depression in the
centre, as against the smooth curves of a bowl used
by 'slurpers' or ravenous spoon-wielders.

SPOONS

The humble spoon was not essential. If it didn't have
to be skewered by the knife, then it could be slurped
– and most Tudors and Stewarts could slurp for their
country. The attitude was, if it wasn't essential,
then don't use it. Only the rich or refined used
anything other than a knife. Today it is traditional
to give children a silver spoon at their christening
but any Tudor child who had a spoon at birth
would have been born into a rather wealthy family.

FORKS

There are many ancient depictions of forks but
we don't know exactly how they were used, as
the Church and the Papacy said that they were
the 'Devil's Claw' and had no place at a Christian
table. If we accept that the fork came into Europe
via Byzantium, not quite the heart of Christianity,
we can understand this outburst.

EARLY FORKS

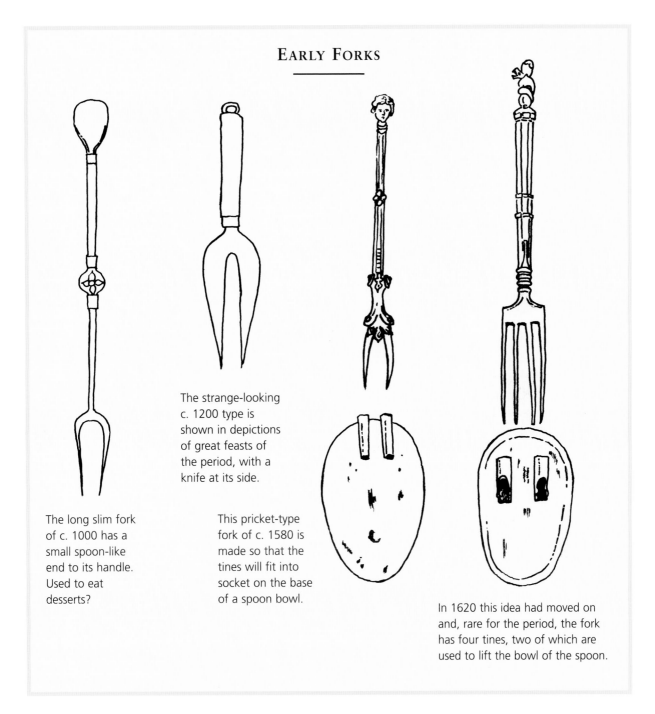

The long slim fork of c. 1000 has a small spoon-like end to its handle. Used to eat desserts?

The strange-looking c. 1200 type is shown in depictions of great feasts of the period, with a knife at its side.

This pricket-type fork of c. 1580 is made so that the tines will fit into socket on the base of a spoon bowl.

In 1620 this idea had moved on and, rare for the period, the fork has four tines, two of which are used to lift the bowl of the spoon.

At first the fork was mainly used by Elizabethan ladies to eat sticky desserts and, just like Georgian tea cups, not something a man would use so much – in fact as late as 1897 the British Navy forbade the use of forks by sailors as effeminate.

So the knife was well in, the spoon was a rich man's tool, but the fork was shunned. A manuscript of 1023 from Montecasino in Italy shows two men conveying food to their mouths with large two-pronged forks in the modern manner.

Small two-pronged forks known as 'prickets' were used by wealthy ladies and some gentlemen in the Tudor period, and it was at this time that there was a rather clever development: the spoon and the fork were made as two parts of the same thing. To achieve this, the tines of the pricket were made so that they could slip into sockets on the underside of the bowl of a spoon, and so be used to convey food to the mouth. This may be the reason that present-day forks are shaped like the bowl of a spoon.

By Jacobean times there are family group portraits showing adults and children at a table, ready to dine. The husband and wife each have a knife, fork and spoon, housed in a rather nice case. Older children have a knife and a two-pronged fork, while smaller children have only a knife. Spoons are grouped in the centre of the table, for anyone who cannot manage with what they have been given. The gradual change in the shape of the spoon from that with a round or pear-shaped bowl to an oval one coincided with the change in the fork, starting in the second half of the sixteenth century and ending at the beginning of the eigtheenth century. So on your tables you can have lots of knives, some spoons, but only a few forks.

I do not know of any period forks on the miniatures market, so the best way to acquire one is buy a spoon and cut or file the bowl to give you tines.

THE PANTOR

From the fourteenth to sixteenth centuries servants tended to the wants of their masters. There was strict ritual in everything and servants had special tools to help them ply their trade. In 1580 the 'pantor' was the officer in charge of the pantry, where the bread was kept (from the French *pain*).

The bread was carried to the table in a fine cloth called a 'port payne', and cut using a special set of knives: a 'chaffer' for cutting large loaves; a 'parer' for trimming cinders and burnt bits off the loaf; a 'trencher' knife used in much the same way as the parer; and a 'mesal' knife for cutting off

▸ **A fine early seventeenth-century cutlery sheath of wood with silver fittings**

the upper crust for use by the upper crust, i.e. the master. The much harder – and quite often burnt – bottom, or lower crust, of the loaf was for use by lesser mortals. So you knew your position in the social strata by the type of bread and the cut you were given.

Most knives used by servants were held not in a block on the kitchen work surface as we do today, but in a special case of leather and/or wood which they kept on their belt. These cases could be quite ornate, a bit like those worn by a highland gentleman in full dress but much, much larger and often to be seen in illustrations of the period.

Find the knives you would like your servant to use, then you can make a case out of two pieces of soft wood. Paint and finish the case to match his livery and attach it to his belt. Most presentation boxes are of rough construction but look good because of the finish. Your knife box should be the same. Remember a 'serving' knife would have a blade which was 9–12in (23–30.5cm) long, looking a bit like a present-day palette knife, so your case has to be quite large.

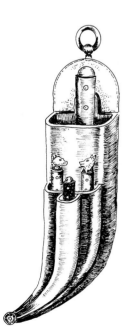

◂ **A sixteenth-century leather case**
This has at least four knives: three small blades, one large, wide blade like a palette knife.

◂ **A Tudor cook**
Proudly wearing as a badge of office his sheath or knife case full of knives, along with his keys to the spice cupboard.
(Drawing after an illustration in *Ein Neu Kochbuch* by Marx Rumpolt.)

TRENCHERS

Not only did the high and mighty get the upper crust but bread baked on the day of the feast was for the lord only. Day-old bread was for his guests, and the household retinue received two- or three-day-old bread. Four-day-old-bread was used for trenchers with the best being made up of four pieces of bread placed together to form a large platter on to which the meal would be served, as depicted in contemporary illustrations. In richer houses these were not eaten, but given to the servants or poor as dole, with just a hint of what their betters had for dinner still lingering on them. In my youth a 'trencher man' was someone who enjoyed his food and we didn't know about its French root a *trenchour*, *trencheoir* or *trenchier*, being the knife used to cut the bread.

By the late sixteenth century, and into the seventeenth century, wooden trenchers were in use, with pewter and so on only used in the best of houses and then on the best of days. A refinement was the roundel, a dessert platter or trencher of wood or ceramic ware, with a decorated surface or surfaces.

The decoration could be painted on, glazed, or printed on paper, then applied to the surface of the roundel, but what is nice is how they were used. Most had mottos or simple verses on them, and when you had eaten the course you had to read it or sing it, much as we do with Christmas crackers.

Queen Elizabeth I had a porcelain set kept in a special box, and no doubt it was only used by close friends. If you wish to see these, you must go to the Pierpoint Library, New York, where they are exhibit M681.

The two drawings overleaf show other roundels – you could emulate these, using transfers or computer-produced images. Some sets illustrated the months of the year and the top roundel is of this type with the following verse: 'November pulls downe hoggs for bacon pork and sowse; housewife save for puddings, goode meate in poor man's howse'. The verse on the upper strawberry roundel runs: 'What better fruite then to live sowe farr from the force of parching heate. What fruite so neere the grownde doth grow, as I and yet so good to eat.'

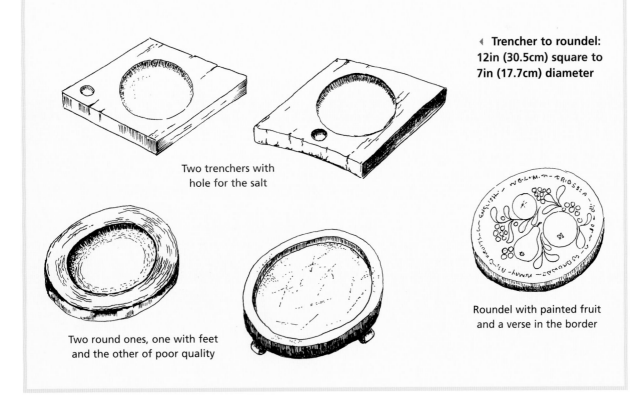

Two trenchers with hole for the salt

Two round ones, one with feet and the other of poor quality

◀ **Trencher to roundel: 12in (30.5cm) square to 7in (17.7cm) diameter**

Roundel with painted fruit and a verse in the border

TRENCHERS

▲ Two roundels

Seasonal images were a popular form of decoration on trenchers. The posh ones – 'roundels' – were used much the same way that we use Christmas crackers, and the inscriptions, rude or otherwise, were sung or read out to fellow revellers.

Top: A Dutch engraving with an English verse. This belonged to an English settler in America, showing the considerable trade in such items.

Bottom: English roundel with verse and picture of strawberries.

BANQUETING HALL ROOM BOX

This room box is based on a number of period houses still existing in the UK, including Washington Old Hall, Chethams Hospital, Manchester and Wortham in Devon. Hall houses were the norm in sixteenth-century England, but this didn't denote status, it was just that the main room of a house, the hall, was open to the roof timbers be it humble or grand. The beams to the roof here are plain dark oak, but many were richly painted and were only 'cleaned' back in the early 1900s.

Both the green and yellow frieze, consisting of dolphins and acanthus leaves, and the mural showing 'The Ages of Man', are based on examples in West Stow Hall, Suffolk. The 'Ages of Man' was one of only a few safe subjects – which included Old Testament themes – that could be displayed in times of religious persecution.

Firebacks prevented the burning of the brick or stone work, as well as acting as a convection heater when the fire was out or low. The fire was also a source of light on dark nights but candles and rush lights were used for other areas.

▼ Chimneypiece

Spices were stored around the fireplace to keep them dry, and sometimes chimneypieces incorporated small alcoves as cupboards to hold the spice boxes; these were kept behind locked doors and supervised by the lady of the house. The late fifteenth/early sixteenth century blue and white pots displayed in the alcoves here were just becoming fashionable, and replaced the spice cupboards.

▲ **The back wall, showing the frieze around top of the wall, and the mural of 'The Ages of Man'**

The panels on the walls were known as 'ceilings' and were often left in wills as 'the ceilings of my hall'. They were not just decorative, but helped to keep the house warm and cut down on draughts through the stonework, hence the term 'ceiling'. Behind the table hangs a large cloth used in much the same way. Most homes had a painted cloth – a canvas painted to look like tapestry – but there could also be a carpet on the table or hanging in place of a tapestry. Only those of a higher social order put carpets on the floor.

Your tapestry can be as rich or as simple as you wish. There are good miniature ones on the market, or you can use a piece of suitable material.

The hall screen below the minstrels' gallery (shown overleaf) was to hide the flow of lesser mortals in and out of the house, and the kitchens from the eyes of the proud owners. Whilst the minstrels' gallery has a door to it, the entrance to the kitchens did not.

The banquet shown, consists of 'umble pie' made from the waste parts of a deer, fresh and glazed fruits provide the desserts, while lamprey eels, snails and other small creatures were side dishes. Pewter tankards and plates are in evidence, but in many even grander homes, wooden platters or trenchers were found.

A 'court cupboard' (Anglo-French for a 'short board for cups') is between the arches of the screens, positioned so that servants could access it and the owner's wealth could be displayed.

Suits of armour were by this time a little old hat and these are replicas of originals now in the Tower of London, being foot combat armour used by Henry VIII in 1520 when he was a fit young man.

▼ Minstrels' gallery (left-hand wall)

Arms were displayed on the minstrels' gallery to impress people of a lower station in life. As your peers had just as good if not better, it took the royal arms or those of some great lord to impress them. Above the mural are the arms of Washington of Washington who later moved to Sulgrave Manor, then to America, coming to rest at Mount Vernon. Is it just coincidence that they consist of stars and stripes?

▲ Tables and chairs

Furniture was good but basic, with the great board or table being the most important piece. It was rare to have a chair and if there was just one, it was for the head of the home, the 'Chairman of the Board', with benches and stools for the other members. Children did not sit at table, but stood on stools or 'crickets' to bring them up to the height of the table.

HOW TO DISTRESS YOUR MODEL

There are paints on the market that give an antique, crackled finish, but most are not suitable for miniatures. I use a dull shade of paint to start with and distress it with a spirit-based stain made in America, which is available in the UK. Take care, as a little will go a long way. Try to wash it off with clean white spirit on a soft rag or brush, taking the darker stain back as far as you wish. Alternatively you could use a darker paint, rather than the spirit stain, but keep it fluid, and don't allow it to dry out until you have the finish you require. Don't worry if you don't get it right first time, as you can paint over it, which, on its own, may give you the result you are looking for.

PROJECT
MAKE THE ROOM BOX

This is a simple box, 18in (46cm) long, 12in (30.5cm) deep and 14½in (37.8cm) high. The main features include the fireplace (see diagrams on pages 103 and 104), the wall panels, and the screen with minstrels' gallery above. When completed, you can protect your model from dust and little hands with a sheet of Perspex or Plexiglass bent through 90° to cover the top and front.

ORDER OF CONSTRUCTION:

1 Assemble the box
2 Lay the floor, be it stone or timber
3 Insert right-hand panel to back wall
4 Insert fireplace
5 Insert left-hand panel to back wall
6 Assemble screens and gallery, but do not fit
7 Mark wall for position of gallery
8 Following the marks, assemble doorways
9 Assemble window in right-hand wall, then add brackets for the tapestry underneath
10 Make a groove in the upper face of the brackets for the tapestry wire to rest in
11 Build, decorate and insert the chimney breast
12 Fit screen and gallery, fit narrow panel if required
13 Fit corbels for roof timbers and tapestry
14 Decorate, then position border
15 Distress your model (see page 135)

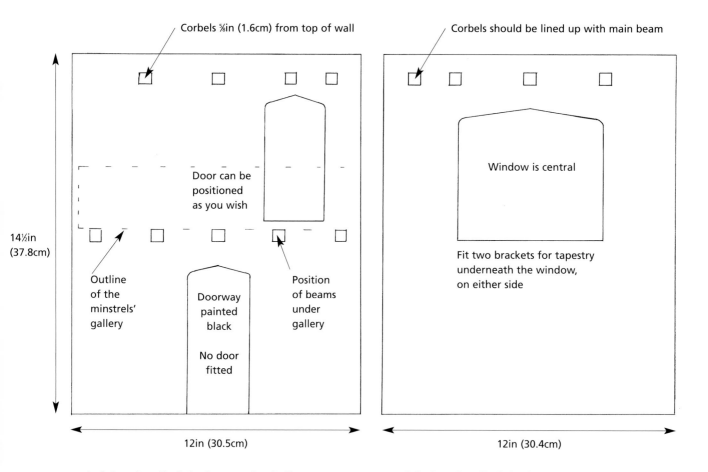

Corbels ⅝in (1.6cm) from top of wall

Corbels should be lined up with main beam

14½in (37.8cm)

Door can be positioned as you wish

Window is central

Outline of the minstrels' gallery

Doorway painted black

No door fitted

Position of beams under gallery

Fit two brackets for tapestry underneath the window, on either side

12in (30.5cm)

12in (30.4cm)

▲ **Left-hand wall of the banqueting hall**

▲ **Right-hand wall of the banqueting hall**

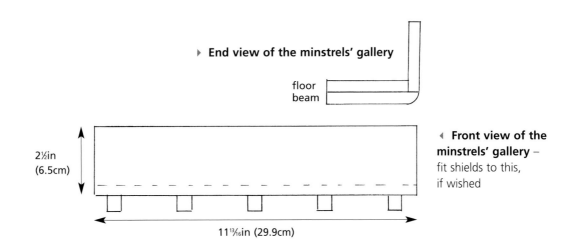

▶ **End view of the minstrels' gallery**

floor
beam

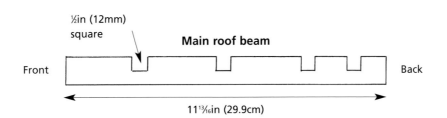

◀ **Front view of the minstrels' gallery** –
fit shields to this,
if wished

2½in
(6.5cm)

11¹³⁄₁₆in (29.9cm)

½in (12mm)
square

Main roof beam

Front

Back

11¹³⁄₁₆in (29.9cm)

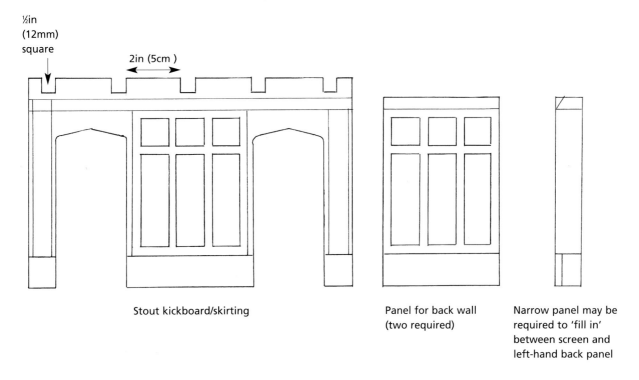

½in
(12mm)
square

2in (5cm)

Stout kickboard/skirting

Panel for back wall
(two required)

Narrow panel may be
required to 'fill in'
between screen and
left-hand back panel

▲ **Screen and panels**

CHAPTER SEVEN

INVENTORIES:

Their Use in Furnishing Your Dolls' House

Information from contemporary written sources, the written record of people who lived and died in the period, can be an invaluable source for the history of a house.

The executors or administrators of the estate of a deceased person were required by an Act of the twenty-first year of Henry VIII's reign to exhibit at the Probate Court two copies of an inventory listing all the worldly goods of the deceased. In practice, these were drawn up after the death, and include particulars of all movable goods and chattels of the deceased person, including personal belongings, clothes and money, as well as the contents of the house. The best examples go through the house room by room, and it is this type that miniaturists will find most helpful. Contact your own County Records Office where you will find the staff interested in your project, or you can go direct to the Public Records Office.

The following inventories will give you an idea of what to expect. It can be a rewarding project on its own to collect drawings and photographs of the type of goods listed, to serve as a useful visual inventory.

EMBLETON VICARAGE, NORTHUMBERLAND, ENGLAND

These are the goods left in 1431 by William Warde, the Vicar of Embleton, who lived in a small fortified house of which only the solar, known as Embleton Tower, survives.

Note that there is only one chair and the table or board stood on trestles.

VI	Oxen	13s.	4d	each
II	Horses	12s.	0d	each
1	Cart	8s.	0d	
1	Cart	5s.	0d	
1	Plough	3s.	8d	
2	Large brewing leedes	£1 4s.	0d	each
1	Large brass pots	13s.	4d	each
1	Small	6s.	4d	
1	Boardcloth and two bowls (high board)	3s.	8d	
1	Boardcloth (sideboard)	1s.	6d	
6	Silver spoons	13s.	4d	
1	Great table for highboard	2s.	8d	

1	Great table for sideboard	1s.	6d
2	Forms	1s.	
2	Pr trestles	1s.	
6	Cushions	3s.	6d
1	Tapestry to ye Hall	11s.	0d
	Bankers to ye Hall	1s.	8d
1	Chair	1s.	6d
6	Garnish vessels	6s.	0d
2	Iron spits 1 @ 1s. 6d plus 10d		
2	Candlesticks	1s.	8d
1	Basin and ewer	5s.	0d
2	Pans 1 @ 5s. 8d 1 at 1s. 10d		
1	Pr tongs		8d
1	Long brand iron	4s.	8d
1	Bed with apparall	£1 0s.	0d
1	Bed (single)	10s.	0d
2	Bolsters	2s.	6d
1	Yetling	6s.	10d
1	Woorte tub	2s.	0d
1	Gylletyng tub	2s.	6d
2	Bowls	1s.	4d

WOODCOTE HOUSE, GREAT BOOKHAM, SURREY, ENGLAND

Henry Wilkins died here, leaving a lot of information about his house in this inventory of 1576.

The Haule Imprimis A table standing one a forme being a stander of the house also one old forme to the table belonginge	2s.	0d
Item a joined cobberd	4s.	0d
Item a potte hanger in the chymny		4d
Item 2 old stolles		1d
Item the paynted clothes [wall hangings] The Kytchen First a cawdran with a bayll like a kettle verie old	2s.	6d
Item a posnett with 3 litle skillets	2s.	6d
Item 8 old platters	2s.	8d
Item 3 dishes		6d
Item 3 sawcers		6d
Item and old grydyron		2d
Item a spitte		3d
Item 2 candlesticks		4d
Item old tubbes		20d
The Chamber First 2 old matrisses		16d
Item 2 paynted testers with clothes about the chamber	2s.	6d
Item 2 blaincketts 2 coverletts	2s.	6d
Item 3 payre of sheatts 2 old clothes	4s.	0d
Item 2 old chests	2s.	8d
Wearing geare First a cote a jurkyne a payre of hoosse a cavis [canuis] short	6s.	4d
Item his purse	2s.	8d
The Barne First by estimacion 20 buschells of wheat and rye	40s.	0d
Item in balie by estimacion	33s.	4d
Item in hay and tarres [tares]	10s.	0d
Item and old phane [winnowing fan] and an old busshell withoute eares		8d
Item in fyve acres of winter corne being what and rye being now soene one the ground	33s.	4d
The Cattle First 3 mayres	33s.	4d
Item one cowe and a bullocke and a weaner of this year	26s.	8d
Item an old cart and thereunto belonging	10s.	0d
Item bacon in the rooffe	2s.	0d
Total 11LL [£11]	11s.	8d

ROTHE HOUSE, KILKENNY, IRELAND

The inventory of John Rothe Fitzpiers has been lost, but the will dated 1619 tells us quite a lot: drawing tables are withdrawing tables; a counter table was used to count money on and gives us the counter in a shop.

The metal work left included 'batry', which is wrought iron, and 'iron' which is cast iron, while the *'seelings of my hall'* are the panels of wood lining a room to keep out draughts. 'Porte corn' was imported corn to be sold to help buy keepsakes. As for 'scabbets', I just don't know!

This is an extract from a will drawn up by a lawyer, which is long and detailed, originally covering nine sheets of closely written paper and reproduced in full in the Reverend William Healy's *History of Kilkenny*, 1893.

Rothe House was a large merchant's house, much like Plas Mawr, Conwy, North Wales, and it is clear that John was trying to make sure that his widow and son could run separate homes within the Rothe mansion.

As in many old wills, the testator's clothes were included in the bequest with William Shee, a son-in-law, having a choice of a *'sigone cloth cloak'* or a gown of *'browne blew collor'*. Keepsakes, mostly signet rings or the money to have one made, are mentioned as well as the *'forgiveness'* of small debts.

ITEMS LISTED IN THE WILL
1/3 of bedstedds, boordes, chairs, stooles and evry other the stuffes, furniture, and utensils …

To my said wife all her jewels of gold and silver and the third part of all my diaps, Holland and Lynin … my tapistrie courlet, and the sey greene hangings, or cwrtyns.

Drawing tables, bedsteads, cupboords livery, cupboord, virginalls, wainscot, seelings of my hall and chambers, benches, long tables, scabbets, ioynts stools, chairs, my great cipresse chest and cipresse counter … Pewter, brasse, batry, iron, beddings of feathers and flocks … plate … cattle … fowerscore bags of porte corne to help them buy jewels.

Hengrave Hall, Suffolk, England

Hengrave Hall was built for Sir Thomas Kytson, a London merchant in 1525–1538, and is externally one of the most impressive houses of the reign of Henry VIII. This inventory was made in 1603, the year Elizabeth died and James Stewart became King.

Items three square boards, with fast frames to them [tables]

Two joyned coobards, made fast to the wainskote [built in]

One long table for a sholven borde with fast frame to it [a 'sholven borde' is a shovel board on which they played push or shove halfpenny]

One other long table, with tressels to it

One piece of wood carved with the Queen's arms

Ten joyned formes for the square borde

One long forme not of joyners work

One great branch of cooper which hangs in the midst of the hall to serve for lights

Four copper-plate candlesticks, iii of them being great and one little, which hangs upon the skreine by ye pantrye

One cradle of iron for the chimney to borne the seacole with

One pier sholve made like a grate to sift the seacole with

One other pier shove and one payer of tongues

Two payr of tables

[Sea-cole was coal brought by ship from Wales or Tyneside.]

In ye Great Chamber
Arras
Carpets
Cushions
Thirty-two stools, joyned

Four chayeres
Curtains
On joyned coobard
One square borde
Lone joyned borde and extension piece [draw-leaf table]
Two long footstools under above
One payer of tables
One seven-fold and one fourfold skreenes
One great copper sesteurne to stand at the coobard
Two payer andyrons
Two payer creepers [small brand irons]
Four copper branches for lights
Two fire sholves, to payer tongues and one fire forke

In ye Gallerye at ye Tower
One billiarde borde with the staves to it of bone and two of wood and 4 balls

This inventory draws a distinction between trestle tables and tables with fixed legs or frames. It also introduces the folding screens with four and seven panels.

Lighting was important and a number of fittings are listed, but do take care and don't make them too grand. It is interesting in that there is a fire basket for the burning of coal but they also burn logs with andirons (also known as spit dogs as they held the roasting meat), and creepers which were used to prevent broken logs creeping forward into the body of the room.

The carpets and cushions point to a comfortable table with the carpet being used like a table cloth. The arras was a tapestry from the town of that name in Artois annexed to the Duchy of Burgundy, but in decline at that time.

ILLUSTRATED EXAMPLES

Seldom will any inventory be complete and it is hard to understand why some items, which were essential in most homes, were overlooked. The most detailed lists come from the homes of the great and good, with scribes eager to show the wealth and standing of their master, rather than being interested in the brew house or the kitchens, the dirty end of domesticity.

The following 'illustrated inventory' is made up of sections from various documents to help give a better overall picture of a house of medium quality.

HALL

We will start with the hall. This could be grand but in most houses it was little more than a room with no floor over it, allowing smoke to rise above the heads of the occupants.

- A tabell [no frame, so assume it is a trestle]
- A round tabell
- Three joined stooles and four crickets [children's stools]
- Two formes
- Three cushions [are these for the three stooles?]
- A banker [cover for a seat]
- Stayne clothes [wall hangings dyed, not painted]
- Cradle of iron for the chimney [coal burning, not logs]
- Shovel like a grate [to sift the ashes]
- Tongues (tongs)
- Wood carved with Queen's arms [richly painted status symbol]
- A coobard with desks [with shelves]
- A livery cupboard [to hold remains of meal to be eaten later]
- Iron pot hanger
- The ceilings [wooden panels to the walls]
- Standard skreene
- Two aquamaniles [animal-shaped water containers for washing of hands – see below right]
- One citern [?]

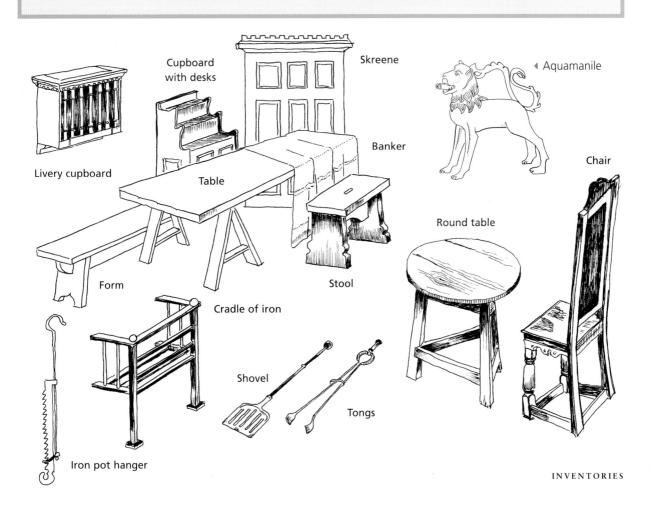

Livery cupboard — Cupboard with desks — Skreene — Aquamanile — Table — Banker — Chair — Form — Stool — Round table — Cradle of iron — Shovel — Tongs — Iron pot hanger

PARLOUR

Next came the parlour, which was a room set aside from the hall and at first intended as an apartment for private conversation. These rooms were more elegant and showy than the hall.

- A board framed [a table with fixed legs]
- One round table [small dropleaf table?]
- Two formes
- Four stooles joined [carpenter made them]

- Presse for painted clothes [chest]
- Joyned bedsted with truckle
- Fether bed [as much a status thing, as the car is to us]

- Chayre
- Bolster
- Coverlet
- Pyllowes
- Close stoole
- Counter [table to count money on]

- Some bookes
- Coffer [small strong-box for the money]
- Chest
- Laver and napry [washstand and towel]

▲ ▶ **Parlour**

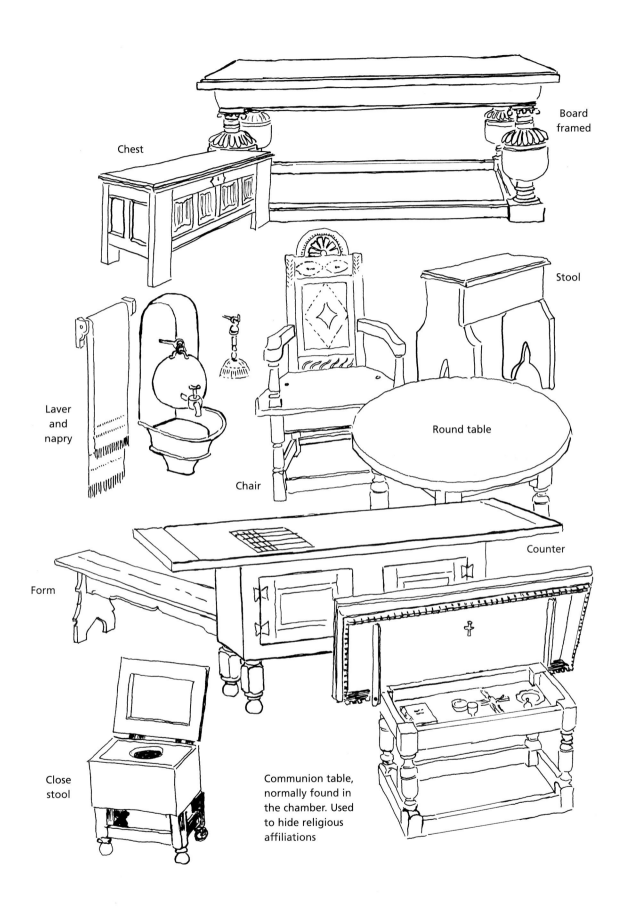

Board
framed

Chest

Stool

Laver
and
napry

Chair

Round table

Form

Counter

Close
stool

Communion table,
normally found in
the chamber. Used
to hide religious
affiliations

KITCHEN

The kitchen is the room most scribes would overlook but was filled with the most interesting things: the 'gylleting tub' could be used for fermenting some stew or ale, or could be used as a trough or tray to hold an animal while the butcher dressed it ready for roasting, and so on.

The brand irons may hide an intended list of the various types of fire dogs used in the kitchen. 'Two chimney cranes' implies an active kitchen which even boasts a spit jack, which was new on the market at this time.

- A cawdran with bayll [cauldron with a handle]
- Two old cardrans
- Posnett
- Skillets
- Platters of wood
- Grydyron
- Spittes
- Spitte jack
- Old tubbes three

- Grinding stone and stand
- Old spoons
- Garnish vessels [jugs, bowls and jars of sauces]
- Gylleting tub [dialect, can be for fermenting or a butcher's trough]
- Brand irons [fire dogs for logs or brands]

- Chimney hooks [pot hangers]
- Two chimney cranes
- Trivets [used for fine cooking]
- Two wooden peles [to put bread in or remove bread from the oven]
- Mawkin, old [mop to clean out the oven]

- Platter car [trolley for dirty dishes]
- Block [chopping block]
- 6 dishes and sasers
- 2 bessums [brooms or brushes]
- Old screene [not required now as they have a spit jack]

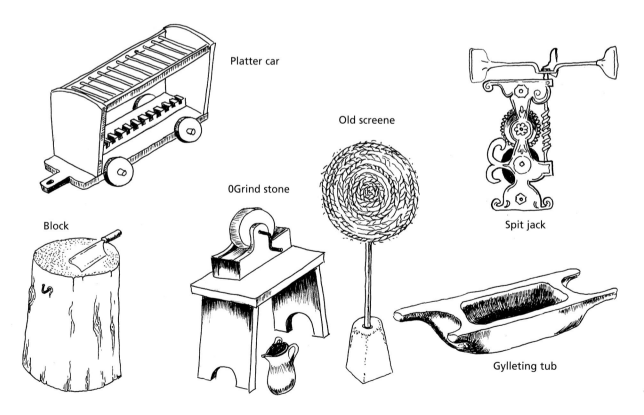

Platter car

Old screene

0Grind stone

Block

Spit jack

Gylleting tub

▲ ▶ **Kitchen**

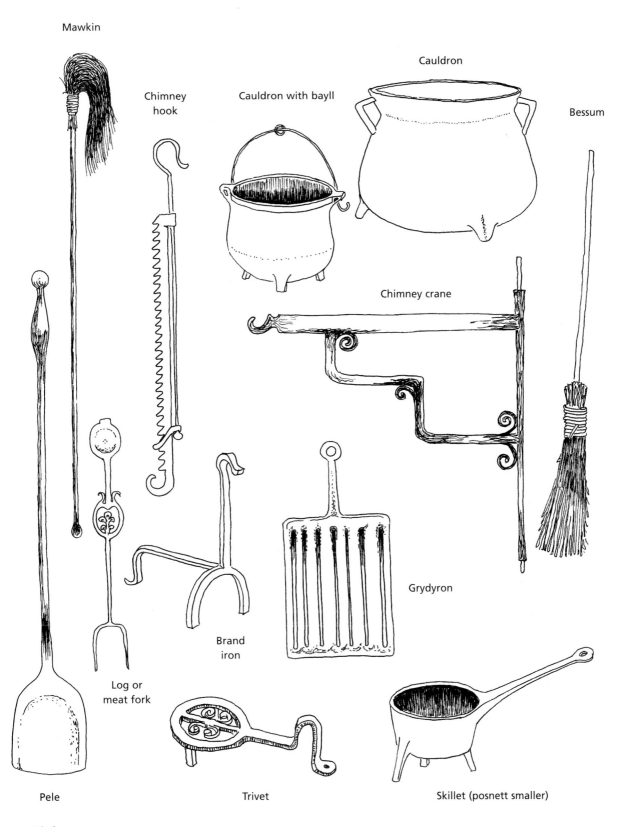

Mawkin

Chimney
hook

Cauldron with bayll

Cauldron

Bessum

Chimney crane

Grydyron

Brand
iron

Log or
meat fork

Pele

Trivet

Skillet (posnett smaller)

▲ Kitchen

CHAMBER

The next room is the chamber, comfortable but not showy, of which there could be more than one.

The fire irons tell us they would burn logs here, but why did they require spit dogs? Footstools indicate that the table was higher than we would use today, and the folding screens were the latest fashion. A 'copper sesteurne' was to hold water and would stand on a small cupboard. The prayer desk shows they had faith, but the communion table tells us it was not safe to boast about it. Shovel boards and even billiard boards can be found in good number at this time.

- Folding table with footstooles under
- Fire shovels and tongs
- Andyrones [spit dogs – out of place here?]
- Creepers [small fire dogs]
- Seven fold and one four-fold skeenes
- Capet [table carpet]
- Arras [tapestry]
- Two cushions
- Two stooles
- Copper branches for lights
- Great coppes sesteurne
- Prayer desk
- Ye communion table
- Shovel board
- Chest

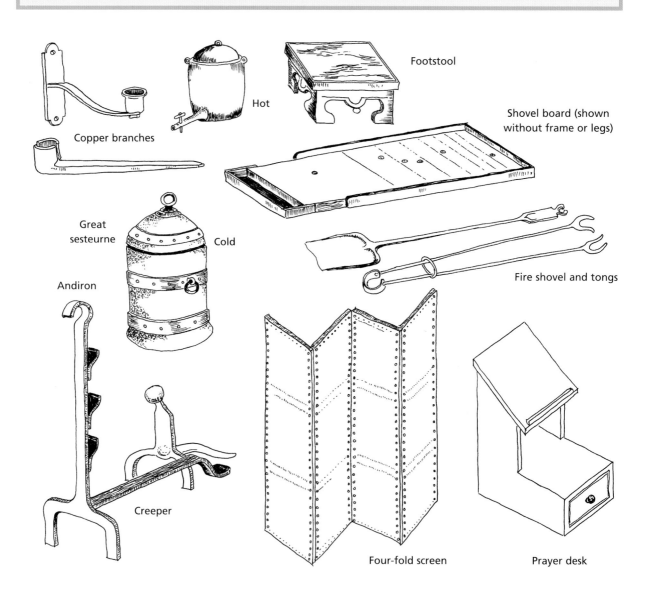

Copper branches

Hot

Footstool

Shovel board (shown without frame or legs)

Great sesteurne

Cold

Fire shovel and tongs

Andiron

Creeper

Four-fold screen

Prayer desk

CHAPTER EIGHT

FURNITURE AND DECORATIONS

The Board • Chests and Cupboards • Bench or Settle
• The Painted House

THE BOARD

In the Tudor period most tables consisted of a pair of trestles with a stout oak board resting on top of them. The trestles were sturdy but simple, with only a few variations of shape or type. Most numerous were the 'comb' type, with only three legs, and the double 'A' (see below). When not in use the board was lifted off its trestles and hung on the wall. Now and again notices for the instruction of the servants were attached, making it a 'notice board'.

So used were the gentry to eating from a board that, when they were out hunting, some unfortunate servant had to carry the board out into the field so that they could either sit with it on their knees, or sit around it.

In the mid-sixteenth century refectory tables came in, with boards fixed to frames and anything from four to fourteen legs. The top of many framed tables has a more ancient look than the legs, as they used the old board of a trestle table as the table top.

▲ **Various trestles** Left: 'comb' type; centre: 'A' frame; right: double 'A' (more shown overleaf).

BOARD ENDS AND TRESTLES

At the top of the illustration three board ends are shown, with holes or handles which were also used to hang them on a wall, and below, various types of trestle that were used between 1350 to 1850.

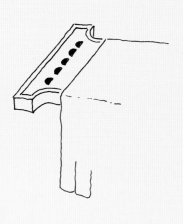 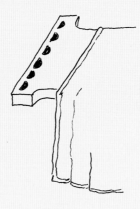 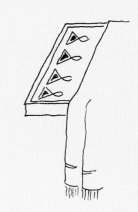

Board ends c. 1500–1670

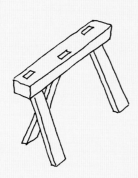  

Further trestles: 'Comb' type   'A' frame   Double 'A'

'A' frame of 1511 – an early three-leg table

'A' frame of 1605

Cake stand/pedestal, used from c. 1640

◀ **The Whitsuntide Cotswold Games**
Detail from a woodcut of 1636 depicting revellers sitting on a groundsheet at the edge of the sports field, with a long board on their knees.

CHAIRMAN OF THE BOARD

Benches and settles were to be found in good number, but most were of crude construction. There were few chairs, and most houses did not even have one. The group of wealthy people who did own chairs was small: one for the master of the house was the most usual, some had two so that the master and his wife could sit in comfort, but only the richest had more than that.

The owner of a single chair was an important man, 'the chairman', and when sitting at his table or board he was 'chairman of the board'. Older children of such an important man would sit on stools or benches, while younger children up to six or seven years old stood on the floor, and the younger ones were put on low stools.

A FAMILY AT TABLE

The drawing below (after a mid-seventeenth-century woodcut) shows a typical arrangement: the father and mother sit on stools with cushions, at the ends of the table, while the older children sit on a bench or form at the back. The youngest child stands on a cricket/cracket next to the mother, while an older one stands on the floor next to the father. Note the use of spoons, but no new-fangled forks, which were only used in grand houses at this time.

These low stools – known as 'crickets' or 'crackets' – were of various heights, and enabled the children to reach the table.

The height of a table has varied with time and with the use it is put to. Today our kitchen work surfaces are higher than the tables we dine at, and the Tudors too had high tables to work on and others to sit at. The best tables were traditionally covered with a white cloth, or a 'table carpet', as carpets were for the most part thought too fine to put on the floor. The five-star treatment gave you a white cloth and, in front of each diner, layers of 'surnapes' – long narrow cloths laid one over another, which were lifted one at a time after each course.

Better 'plate' was not always used, but would be put on display. Henry VIII displayed twelve shelves or desks of gold plate at his feasts; Cardinal Wolsey had six desks of the same, and these were fenced off from the milling throng so that *'no man might come nigh it'*; dukes were permitted four or five desks; lesser noblemen three desks; knights banneret two desks; while ordinary gentlemen were allowed just one desk.

One piece that was used was the great salt, an ornate silver or gilt piece with feet. It was tall and had an ornate lid, cap or canopy but could be almost any shape. This was the first item set on the table so you either sat at or below the salt, depending on your status. These treasures were displayed on fine pieces of furniture.

EXTENDING AND FOLDING TABLES

Not everyone had room for a refectory table, so tables that reduced or extended became common towards the end of our period. Variations were numerous, and included the gate-leg, drop-leaf and folding table. While they could be the only table in a Jacobean house, in the Tudor period they would mainly be used as side tables.

▸ **Drop-leaf table**

▸ Folding Table

The top extends when opened, and is simply supported by stout iron hinges without the aid of lopers or gates. If you wish to make a table like this, make a frame and then set the largest hinges you can find into the sections of the table top.

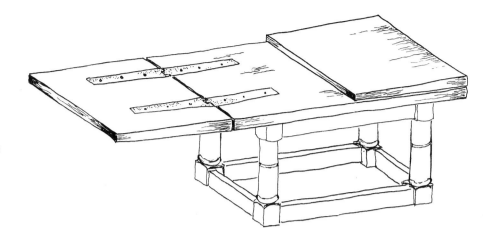

◂ Underside of drop-leaf table

Shows lopers, which support the table top.

▸ **Gate-leg table**

▸ **Underside of gate-leg table**

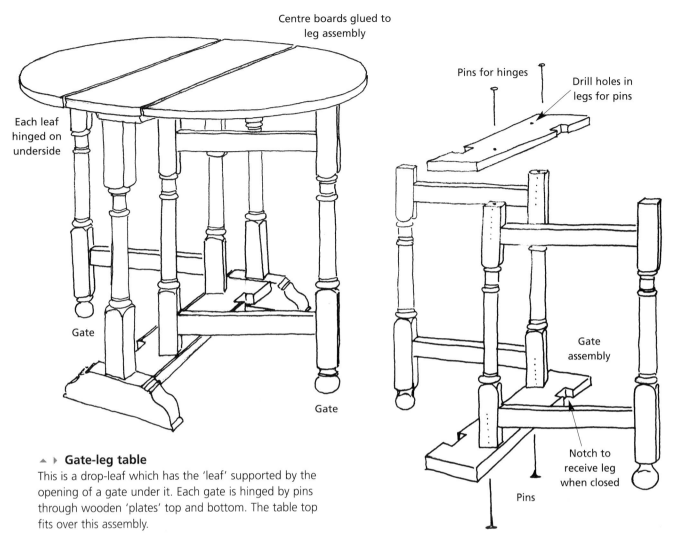

Centre boards glued to leg assembly

Each leaf hinged on underside

Gate

Gate

Pins for hinges

Drill holes in legs for pins

Gate assembly

Notch to receive leg when closed

Pins

▲ ▶ Gate-leg table

This is a drop-leaf which has the 'leaf' supported by the opening of a gate under it. Each gate is hinged by pins through wooden 'plates' top and bottom. The table top fits over this assembly.

◀ Drop-leaf table

Not all supports had legs forming the end of the 'gate'.

CHESTS AND CUPBOARDS

These were the safes of their day and, with many of the early ones, it is easy to see where the term 'trunk' used to describe them originated. The double chest (right) is carved out of a piece of a tree trunk just under 8ft (2.44m) long, which was squared, then hollowed out to give two compartments with walls of 3in (7.5cm) thick. The two lids do not overlap the top of the chest but sink into rebates. The whole was then bound with iron straps and secured with five locks prior to being built into a stone wall which accounts for the rot at its back.

Items made out of part of a tree trunk were not readily portable, yet the term 'trunk' now refers to a portable chest and the chest developed into the chest of drawers, c. 1650. At first drawers were built into the bottom of a chest, then slowly more were fitted to fill the available space and the lid was no longer required. Others developed as a cupboard, with boxes or drawing boxes originally called 'tills', and shopkeepers still keep money in a till.

At Little Moreton Hall, Congleton, Cheshire, there is a sixteenth-century 'Cubborde of Boxes' which was used to hold dried fruit, walnuts, almonds, rice and sugar, and so on, which were of such great value they had to be kept under lock and key.

This locking away of spices was normal, but the 'Cubborde of Boxes' was unusual for this period.

In the late sixteenth century and early seventeenth century some fine chests were being made with painted or carved panels. Most that survive have lost their paintwork and are the dark oak beloved of the Edwardians, who were largely to blame for the removal of much early paint. Be bold, put the paint back on your chest, but don't make it too bright, as the number of pigments they had was small.

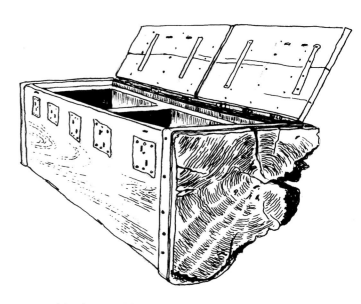

▲ **Double chest, with two lids, c. 1550**

▶ **Iron chest, 1579**
This chest, sunk into a log, was intended from the outset to hold small but valuable items or offerings in a church. The underside of the lid has an inscription that tells us that it was made for John Welsted in 1579, the 21st year of the reign of Queen Elizabeth Regina.

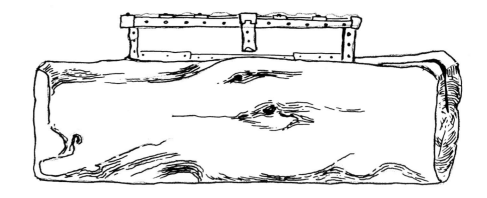

CHESTS FROM THE 'MARY ROSE'

Henry VIII bought new ships to aid his wars against the French, including The Virgin Mary, which was his pride and joy. Henry, Catherine of Aragon and his sister Mary (one-time Queen of France but now married to the Duke of Suffolk) attended the launching at Woolwich. Mary named the ship the *Virgin Mary* but it was always known as the *Mary Rose*.

In the summer of 1545 Henry was dining on board the *Mary Rose* when the French fleet appeared and the *Mary Rose*, less Henry, went into action. The French withdrew, having found an armada of 80 ships sailing against them, but when the *Mary Rose* was returning to harbour she capsized and sank with the loss of all but 30 of her complement of 500. She was raised in 1982 when a treasure trove of domestic paraphernalia was found, unseen since the 19th July 1545. Numerous chests were found, including the two below.

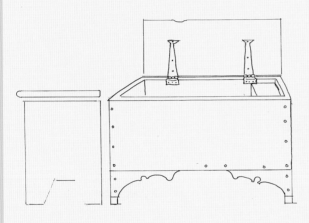

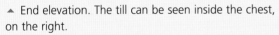

▲ End elevation. The till can be seen inside the chest, on the right.

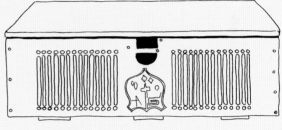

▲ Chest of the Master Gunner on the *Mary Rose*, 1510–45.

◀ **Bishop of Durham chest**
This fine board chest was made for Richard de Bury, one-time Bishop of Durham. The armorial decoration on the inside of the lid can only hint at how fine this was when the decoration still existed on its outer surfaces. The date of construction is mid-fourteenth century.

BENCH OR SETTLE

All forms of seat have evolved from the chest over the years, and early pieces had a locker underneath the seat. The settle is a long chair, which has the distinct characteristics of having arms and being able to accommodate several people. It can be high or low backed.

The oldest settle in the UK is that in Winchester Cathedral, which is thought to be medieval. Other early settles had open backs and a footrest the full length of the seat. Many fifteenth-century manuscript illustrations of these show them with their back to the fire. Others are shown mounted on a dais or low platform.

Wall-mounted settles were found in inns and churches but by the end of the seventeenth century they were much more comfortable, the seat being strung like a bed, and the settee was born. By our standards these were still uncomfortable but were a great improvement on a log.

◄ ▲ Court chairs
The word 'court' did not give a chair status, if anything it reduced it in rank, as it is Anglo-French for 'short'. However, three court chairs grouped together, could form a short settle at a rich man's table.

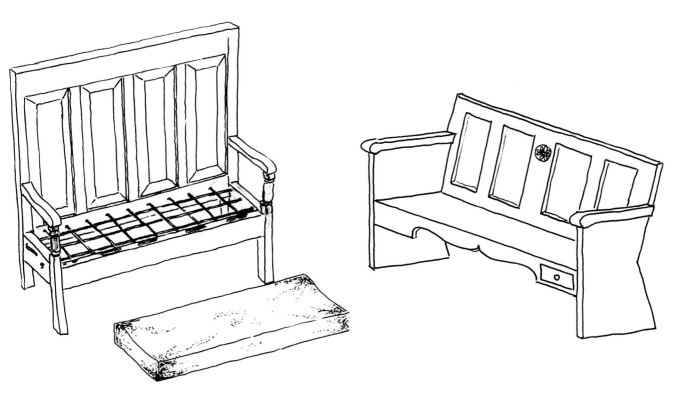

▲ **Mid-seventeenth century**
A move towards comfort – a strong seat, with cushion.

▲ **Seventeenth-century settle**
This one has a drawer underneath.

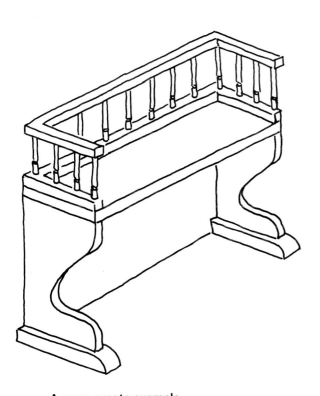

▲ **A more ornate example**
But with no greater comfort.

▲ **Seventeenth-century oak settle**
With a folding table in the back.

THE KNOLE SETTEE

The famous sofa, below, known as 'the Knole settee', was – along with a lot of the furniture at Knole House in Kent – purchased, purloined, acquired or otherwise removed from one of the Royal palaces by one of a number of Sackvilles who held the position of Lord Chamberlain. A sofa was a seat-like dais on which a grand official would sit cross-legged in his audience hall. Catherine of Braganza, Queen of Charles II, so liked the idea she had one made to fit under a canopy, or baldacchino, where she received guests in one of her private rooms.

The Knole came on to the scene in Britain c. 1660. It had adjustable, upholstered arms to give the reclining Queen greater comfort. The arms were adjusted by ratchets of *iron worke double gilt used about the couche*. Modern ones are based more on the Mediterranean version, which has sides or arms held in the position required by tasselled cords tied around large finials. It was not in everyday use in the UK until c. 1900.

In the early seventeenth century things improved further, with a piece of furniture to recline on known as a sofa.

The drawings below and on the previous page are produced to give the basic outline to inspire you to make the piece of your choice. They also show how furniture changed from simple clean lines to the richness of the later seventeenth century.

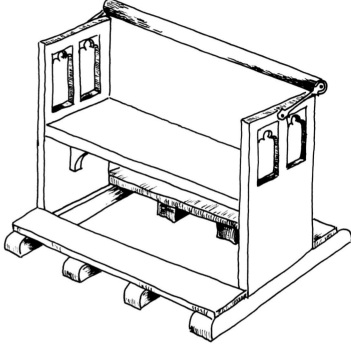

▲ **A Dutch settle**
This has a footrest and the back of the seat is held by a metal hinge so that the sitter can face in either direction.

THE PAINTED HOUSE

Our houses are part of a huge communal picture which we are able to change, but the pressures towards conformity have nearly always been stronger than the desire to go it alone, to stand out as an individual. Due to this conditioning we can all point to houses that don't fit in, and wonder why they were allowed. We may not fully understand it, but we know that there is an acceptable norm for the area we live in, a regional style.

The quality of paint used varied for different sides of the house, depending on exposure to the elements: more valuable oil paint was used for the colours on the south side to combat the heat of the sun, while on the colder north side more body was given to the paint to prevent frost damage. Most early paints would only last one or two years and had to be protected by overhanging eaves and pentice boards.

Stout oak doors of the period were treated with a mixture of oil and varnish to prevent marking, whereas the main timbers only required protection where they came into contact with the ground, and here they were burnt or charred a little. The strong black and white tradition of the British Isles dates, only, from the mid-eighteenth century and is not Tudor at all, since black paint suitable for external use was not available until then.

In areas where stone – or indeed mud – was the building material of choice, it was usual to paint the small area of wall around the doorway white, and to leave that used by the animals in its natural state. Higher up the social scale again, the part of the house used to house the animals was left in its natural state, while the remainder – not just the door – was painted white. It is only in the north-west of England, parts of Scotland and the west of Ireland that adventurous colours were used, and still are, in a way that sits comfortably with the environment.

Unpainted buildings with brick infill to the timbers can be found in areas such as East Yorkshire, East Anglia, the Welsh Boarders, Hampshire and Avon. Lancashire and Cheshire have bold black woodwork against the white infill, while in East Anglia the timbers are grey with shades of red on the plaster, yet 'Constable Country' favours yellows or apricot, in fact all the buffs. On the island of Anglesey in Wales, then down the Llyn Peninsula and as far south as North Pembroke, ochre and pink colour washes are found in contrast to the cob houses of west Wales, which are whitewashed.

PAINT RECIPES

For many centuries paints were used to decorate, rather than protect, the fabric of the house, to make it a place of comfort or protection in a wild untamed landscape. One of the earliest and easiest colours to make was white, which was made using chalk dust mixed with milk and size. The size was made by boiling animal skins. It was used as a binding agent, and white still accounts for over 50 per cent of all exterior decoration.

Other colours which were easy to make used such ingredients as bullocks' blood, soot and regional pigments such as yellow ochre from Oxfordshire, umber from Cornwall and red ochre from Devon, which all had the disadvantage of being a bit on the dull side. Later, merlin-like, men experimented with these basic colours and by mid-medieval times we had recipes producing red, white and yellow from lead, green from copper, and vermillion from sulphur and quicksilver.

The recipes were closely guarded secrets, but John Prizeman in his book *Your House: The Outside View* quotes a recipe for a limewash tempora distemper of 1356 as *'two parts of chalk dust to one of size the size made from boiled strips of leather with at various stages the addition of egg yolks, milk, beer, wine and salt'*. In later recipes potatoes were an important ingredient.

INTERIOR DECORATION: FRIEZES AND PAINTED CEILINGS

There is an excellent collection of Tudor painted decoration, made by the use of stencils, in the Saffron Walden Museum, Essex, but many were much more elaborate. At least one example, the frieze in the Great Chamber of Gilling Castle, North Yorkshire, was much admired by William Morris and inspired the illuminated pages in his version of Chaucer's *The Canterbury Tales*, printed at the Kelmscott Press. This frieze is painted in deep colours direct on to the plaster and has a row of what for 1585 were realistic trees hung with 370 coats of arms. The scene is enlivened by two panels showing ladies and gentlemen playing musical instruments against the backdrop of rich foliage.

Most friezes were not as rich as this, being little more than outline drawings in brown or black, and only a small amount of colour. The diagrams reproduced here can be copied and printed in any colour or size you want, then applied direct to the walls of your dolls' house.

In Scotland the painted ceiling comes into its own, even though examples do exist in other parts of Britain.

▲ **Gladstone's Land, Edinburgh, Scotland**
These drawings of flower-filled vases under bold arches, are based on a frieze in a bedroom, dated c. 1600.

▲ **Frieze, West Stow Hall, Suffolk, England**
Just as bold but more Italianate are these dolphins painted on the walls of a room above the gatehouse, c. 1530.

Painted ceilings take many forms, but at Crathes Castle, Aberdeenshire is an example of one peculiar to that area (see pages 164–5).

Not all paintings were so fine and not all verse aimed at the education of the family. At Montacute House, Somerset there is a simple lament '*A nice wife and a back doore, oft marketh a rich man poore*'. At Owengate, in the city of Durham, there was recently found a painted ceiling much lower down the social scale than Crathes and crude in construction, so they were not all in fine houses. Whether walls are of timber or plaster they could be treated in much the same way, and at Cross Farm, Westhay, Somerset, England, there is a wooden screen of stud and plank construction. The screen was painted c. 1550–1600, the artist or decorator applying his paint quite arbitrarily, with little regard for the stud and plank construction. The result is one of the most remarkable survivals of the Tudor period.

▾ **'The Ages of Man', West Stow Hall, Suffolk, England**
When it came to murals you had to be careful, as you could find yourself in trouble in times of religious persecution. Safe subjects included Old Testament themes, the virtues and moral themes.

Thus do I all the day   Thus do I while I may   Thus did I while I might   Good Lord will this last forever

▴ **Delgatie Castle, Aberdeenshire, Scotland**
This simple and elegant early seventeenth-century frieze could be taken for Georgian.

Firle Place, Sussex, England (Early Tudor)

This early Tudor house has been the home of the Gage family for more than 500 years. The drawing above is after an elaborate decorative frieze – a tempera decoration in the style of carved panelling – depicting boys and girls in grass skirts among foliage, holding up shields with the arms of Gage and Guldeford Quartery. You could use this outline to make a frieze for your dolls' house, perhaps incorporating your own coat of arms, or a badge or emblem that is a pun on your family name.

Common pigments such as white and lampblack are shown in small amounts, but the more expensive blends of verdigris were used in a predominant role. Could this be a statement of 'wealth', with the pigments all easy to find but with the most expensive being used ostentatiously? With examples like this you don't have to be a great artist. Just be bold and move beyond the fashionable Jacobean oak used by most miniaturists and brighten up your house just as they did.

There would be much more of this kind of work left if it had been more durable but, sorry to say, our misguided Edwardian forbears had a thing about 'cleaning' their woodwork to show off the nature of the wood. This was an 'Arts and Crafts' notion, which removed much of the original paintwork and along with it much of the charm of Tudor and Jacobean houses.

▶ **Great Chamber, Hardwick Hall, Derbyshire, England**
Hardwick Hall is rich in Tudor decor of all sorts and here is a drawing after an example of strapwork, which could be of applied plaster or painted on in outline. The actual frieze is painted, and has period prints pasted in the panels. This use of prints developed into the print rooms of the Georgian era.

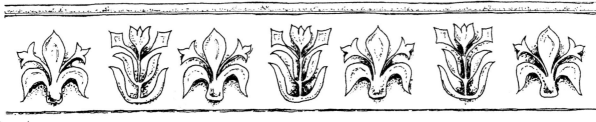

Lavenham

Hadleigh

Yoxford

Yoxford

Clare

▲ **Friezes in Suffolk, England**

THE GREAT HALL, CRAIGIEVAR, SCOTLAND, 1610–26

At this most Scottish of houses, a bold Stuart display of arms is enhanced by medallion portraits of the Nine Worthies on the ceiling. These appear in almost every renaissance palace in Europe from the Rhine to the Doure, the Loire to the Arno, and are found in many guises: carved oak roundel at Falkirk, wooden panels at Craigston, and in many painted ceilings, such as Crathes. Decorative pendants such as these were commonly found in Elizabethan country houses as well as the medallion portraits of the Muses.

PAINTED CEILING, MUSES ROOM, CRATHES CASTLE, ABERDEENSHIRE, SCOTLAND

The muses were the children of Jupiter, and they presided over and inspired music, poetry, dancing and the liberal arts. On the central panel the arms of Katherine Gordon of Lesmoir, wife of Alexander Burnett, are painted, indicating that the room was used as her own private apartment, or withdrawing room. The beams between the painted panels have scrollwork decoration on their underside, while on their sides they have quatrain stanzas of Scots verse related to the virtues and muses close by.

If you would like to have a ceiling like this in your dolls' house, see the project overleaf.

PROJECT
PAINT A MINIATURE CEILING

To make and paint your own miniature ceiling like the one at Crathes Castle, photocopy this outline (reducing or enlarging it as necessary, to fit your dolls' house), then paint it with acrylics using the authentic strong, vibrant colours shown on the previous page. You can print the outline direct on to a sheet of wooden flooring or wood-grained paper, but plain paper would do. If wood flooring is used, treat it with a sealant – to prevent the colours running with the grain of the planking – prior to printing and painting. Whichever you choose, paint it first, then mount it on to a ready-made ceiling prior to fitting the beams.

DUMMY BOARDS

For a long time it was thought that dummy boards were used in much the same way as fire screens, being positioned in front of a fierce fire to protect the occupants of the room. It is now thought that their construction was such that they could not have resisted the constant heat of the fire, and that they served instead to conceal the fireplace, and make a house look inhabited when it was not in use. They were of simple construction and usually painted on to primed boards. You can make dummy boards quite simply, by cutting up suitable postcards and slotting them into notched brackets, so that they stand up.

CHAPTER NINE

THE NEXT GENERATION

Toys • Walking Aids for Babies • High Chairs

The equipment, toys and furniture used by children are never listed in inventories. Was it that these items were not so well made as adult furnishings and have perished, or that inventories listed the goods of older people, beyond the childbearing age, who had passed the items on? Whatever the reason, we have to look further for evidence. Paintings of the period tend to show the rich, woodcuts show a little wider strata of the population, but it is literature that tells us much more.

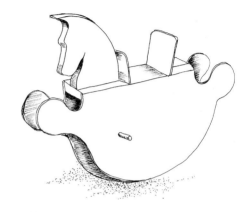

▲ **Sixteenth-century rocking horse**

TOYS

Not many toys survive, although they can be found in period illustrations. A basic rocking horse is shown on the right. This would be for a child from a wealthy family. It is of simple construction, but it could be painted if you wished. The two semi-circular sides are kept apart by spacers, and there is a carved horse's head and a seat on the top. Some had footrests, but not all.

There were also trumpets; push-along horses; ceramic or wooden dolls; balls of leather or an animal's bladder; swords and many variations of dice and board games. Playing cards were for the rich at this time.

Push-along horses looked much like the ones used by children c. 1920, with the animal having a stout wooden body, and spindly legs mounted on a wheeled platform. So go to it, and give your child the best you can!

WALKING AIDS FOR BABIES

As ever, the offspring of the rich were well looked after, while the child of a peasant was required in the field tomorrow and was encouraged to walk much sooner than we would expect today. Various 'aids' were employed to develop the sturdy legs, and different versions of the baby runner were still to be found in reasonable numbers. This consisted of a slim post pivoted by metal pins in the floor and overhead beams of a room.

▲ **Baby runners**

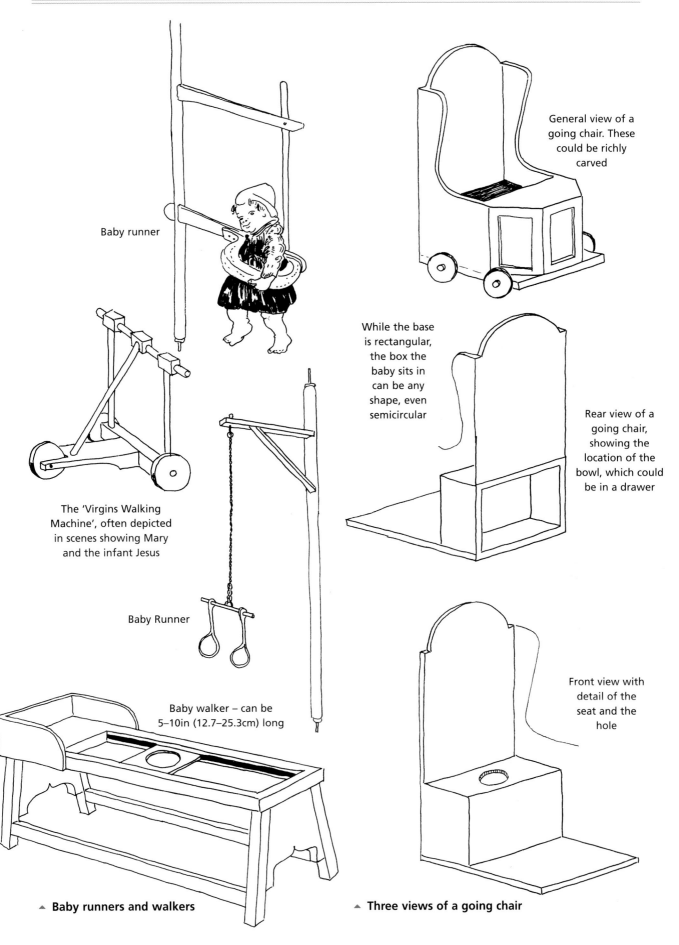

Baby runner

The 'Virgins Walking Machine', often depicted in scenes showing Mary and the infant Jesus

Baby Runner

Baby walker – can be 5–10in (12.7–25.3cm) long

General view of a going chair. These could be richly carved

While the base is rectangular, the box the baby sits in can be any shape, even semicircular

Rear view of a going chair, showing the location of the bowl, which could be in a drawer

Front view with detail of the seat and the hole

▲ **Baby runners and walkers**

▲ **Three views of a going chair**

Attached to this were various forms of hoop, belts and straps which held the child, while allowing its feet to touch the floor and walk round and round and round. There were others, not quite so comfortable, which held the infant under the arms, rather than the midriff. These are all simple to make and do not take up much space.

Baby walkers, on the other hand, could be 10ft (305cm) long, but most were half that. A long narrow frame in which a sliding panel was fixed was supported on short legs, allowing a child's feet to touch the floor when secured in a round hole in the sliding panel. Some of these walkers had a small bench or tray at one end, for food or toys.

Higher up the social scale children used 'going chairs', which also came in two main types: first there was a box on wheels with a seat in it and – sometimes – a tray or bench in front; the other variation had a wooden bowl under the seat to receive bodily fluids – then, as now, when you had to go you had to go and you had a going chair. Some of these pieces are quite simple but others are more ornate.

HIGH CHAIRS

High chairs have been with us for a long time, but early examples look as if they are more for posture-correction than for comfort. At first there was no bar to hold the baby in, but some have holes in the sides, or arms to allow it to be secured by cords, and so on. Later, a simple drop-bar hinged at one side was introduced, and last of all came the tray for food or toys.

Older children were not so lucky: they did not sit at the table, but stood on stools of various heights to bring them up to the height of the table, as shown in my drawing based on a period woodcut on page 149. The stools were known as 'crickets' or 'crackets', depending on the local dialect. Slightly older children – say eight or nine to teenage – sat on a stool. Now that's grown-up.

▾ **A miniature high chair**
Made using the frame of an adult's chair, with a smaller one mounted on top. As the seat was too deep for a child, a footrest was added at the front. This example comes from Gloucestershire and is early seventeenth-century Jacobean. Have you got a redundant chair you could use in this way?

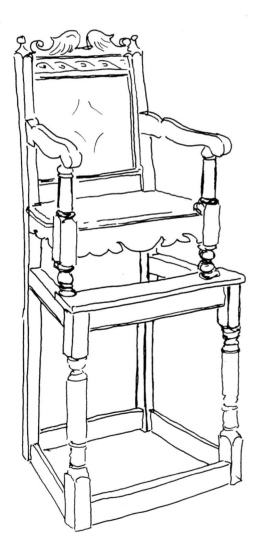

▾ **A simple high chair**

CHAPTER TEN

MISCELLANEOUS ITEMS

Telling the Time: Candles, Clocks and Sundials • Musical Instruments

TELLING THE TIME

According to the chronicler Asser, King Alfred the Great (871–99) marked the passing time by using beeswax candles, banded at twelve regular intervals, a method also recorded in other parts of Europe. The English preferred the four-hour candle, regulated by being allowed to burn to extinction within the protection of a draught-free horn lantern.

In Jacobean auction houses they would 'sell by the candle' by inserting a pin or nail into the side of a candle, about 1in (2.5cm) from the top; the bidding started as soon as the candle was lit, and the winner was the last one to bid before the nail fell out. This was also known as 'selling by the inch'.

PROJECT
MAKE MINIATURE CANDLES

To replicate candles, whether tall and slim, or short and fat, paint suitable lengths of bought dowel, then drip real wax on for that messy look, or add blobs of glue and paint to simulate dripping wax once the glue has set.

So what you have in your dolls' house depends on how grand it is. Most would have nothing, but many would have a sundial. Houses at the heart of a rich estate would have a bell and palaces would have ornate instruments. Towards the end of the sixteenth century and the start of the seventeenth, drum clocks would be on tables and there were brass portable clocks. Sand-glass timers of many durational runs were available and candles were marked off with banding on nails.

CLOCKS

Clocks derived from the French *cloche* – a bell without hands or pointers – which simply rang out over the meadows from church towers, announcing the canonical hours from prime to vespers. The first known domestic clock in England, still unaltered and in its original position, is in the National Trust property at Cotehele, Cornwall. Installed in 1485–9 for Sir Richard Edgcumbe, it has no face and no pointers but indicated the time by simply striking a bell.

As late as the mid-sixteenth century many people worked an 'artificial' day, daylight being divided into 12 'hours' of equal length, with the actual duration of the hour varying from summer to winter. This was all well and good for the village church, but the monk in his monastery employed a water clock, and it was they who introduced mechanical clocks so that for some, at least, the day could be divided into 24 hours of equal duration.

The first truly portable clock came from Nuremberg about 1510 and Mary Queen of Scots had a French watch which was unearthed in 1817 by a mole digging for worms on Queen's Mire, which was part of her route to and from Hermitage Castle.

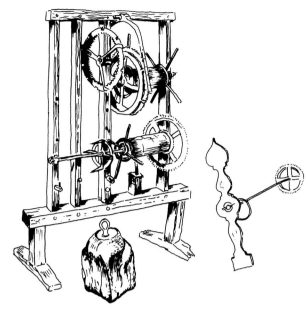

▲ Clock at Belsay Castle, Northumberland, England
The weights were raised and the clock wound up by means of spoke-like handles projecting radially from each of its two barrels. Originally it did not have a pendulum but one was contrived for it as late as 1800, yet the clock is c. 1620. If building one in miniature, the works of a clockwork spit jack can be used as they were all made by the same craftsman.

The family of the shepherd who found the watch took it to South Africa and subsequently donated it to Mary Queen of Scots House, Jedburgh, Roxburghshire, Scotland. In August 1987 it was stolen but just over a year later it was returned in a package with a Canadian postmark. A very portable clock.

The 'clock' of Salisbury Cathedral, Wiltshire, was built in 1386, but never had a face, only striking a bell, while that from Wells Cathedral, Somerset had a 24-hour dial. Its works are now in the Science Museum, London. Both clocks are thought to be the work of Mr Lightfoot, who was Johannes Lietuyt, one of three 'orlogiers' from Delft who were invited to England by Edward III to build a movement for his new tower at Westminster.

The first dial put on display for public use was that of Magdalene College, Oxford. At Hampton Court Palace there is a fine astronomical clock made in 1540 for Henry VIII which indicates the hour, the month, the day of the month, number of days since the year began, the phases of the moon and the time of high water at London Bridge – all a bit too much if you just want to know if it is teatime yet.

SUNDIALS

Sundials were much used by the clergy and to ornament the courts and gardens of fine houses.

In the Privy Garden at Hampton Court there were two sundials '*of remarkable sophistication and complication*'. In 1625 a 'horizontal dyall' on a great pillar of Portland stone was made and furnished with fourteen engraved brass gnomons. To further show the court's love of such toys, in 1631–2 a mathematician called John Marr designed and constructed nine large hemispherical dials and seven large plain dials for the Portland stone base.

Traditionally, on the island of Jersey, many sundials were attached to, or carved into, chimneys. At Les Corvées, Mont Pinel, Jersey, behind the house (not on the chimney) is a most unusual sundial mounted horizontally on a miniature tower about 8ft (2.5m) high. The dial is 23in (58.5cm) in diameter and 3½in (8.9cm) thick; it has Roman numerals and is thought to be late sixteenthth century. Similar ones exist on the island at Gorey Castle and Hamptonne.

There are many smaller devices to be found, particularly in Scotland, which are more suited to the miniaturist, which could be used to decorate a special house.

▲ Lectern sundial
Was the nose a gnomon?

The Great Sundial, Madeley Court, Shropshire, England

Some sundials are large, complicated and so ornate they look like the creation of a wizard. This one (right), consists of a 4ft (1.25m) cube of stone resting on stout drum legs, 15in (38cm) high and capped by a dome 15in (38cm) high that is 30in (76cm) diameter. The whole thing sat on a 16ft (5m) diameter plinth which rose by three 8in (20cm) high steps. I give all these measurements because to the wizards amongst you they could be of vital importance. The north face of the cube is plain, the others covered with hollows, round, square, triangular and shield-shaped. The last, no doubt, once contained the coat of arms of the owner and his wife. The larger hollows have the sockets in which the gnomons were fixed. The little hollows on all three sides help to tell the hour, and the instrument can also be used for finding the position of the moon in relation to the planets.

WATER CLOCKS OR CLEPSYDRA

Sundials measure time variably, but water clocks measured the passing of time with a constant flow, even in the dark. Most were not too complicated, producing a steady flow or drip of water from a reservoir; as the water level changed, the time was read by the marks exposed.

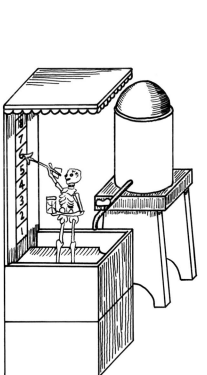

◁ **Water Clock – type No. 1 (1634)**
Water flowing from a reservoir fills another vessel. There is a floating platform with a pointer to indicate on a scale of hours what time it is (see project overleaf).

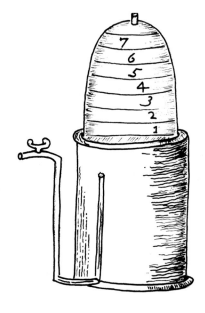

◁ **Water Clock – type No. 2 (1634)**
A vessel with a tiny hole in its top sinks, as the air escapes from it, into a tank of water. The surface of the sinking vessel is marked in hours, noted by an observant time-keeper.

PROJECT
MAKE A WATER CLOCK

Water clocks are not small, but are simple to make and would brighten any period room. The size is, to a large extent, dictated by the figure used to point the hours, which can be anything from a knight on horseback, as shown below, to the bag of bones shown in the drawing on the previous page.

The model shown here is in 1/12 scale. To make this model, build a simple box using ⅛in (3mm) thick wood, and make the back much higher than the other three sides. The depth of the reservoir should be such that the pointer is at 'zero' when empty, but at '8' when full.

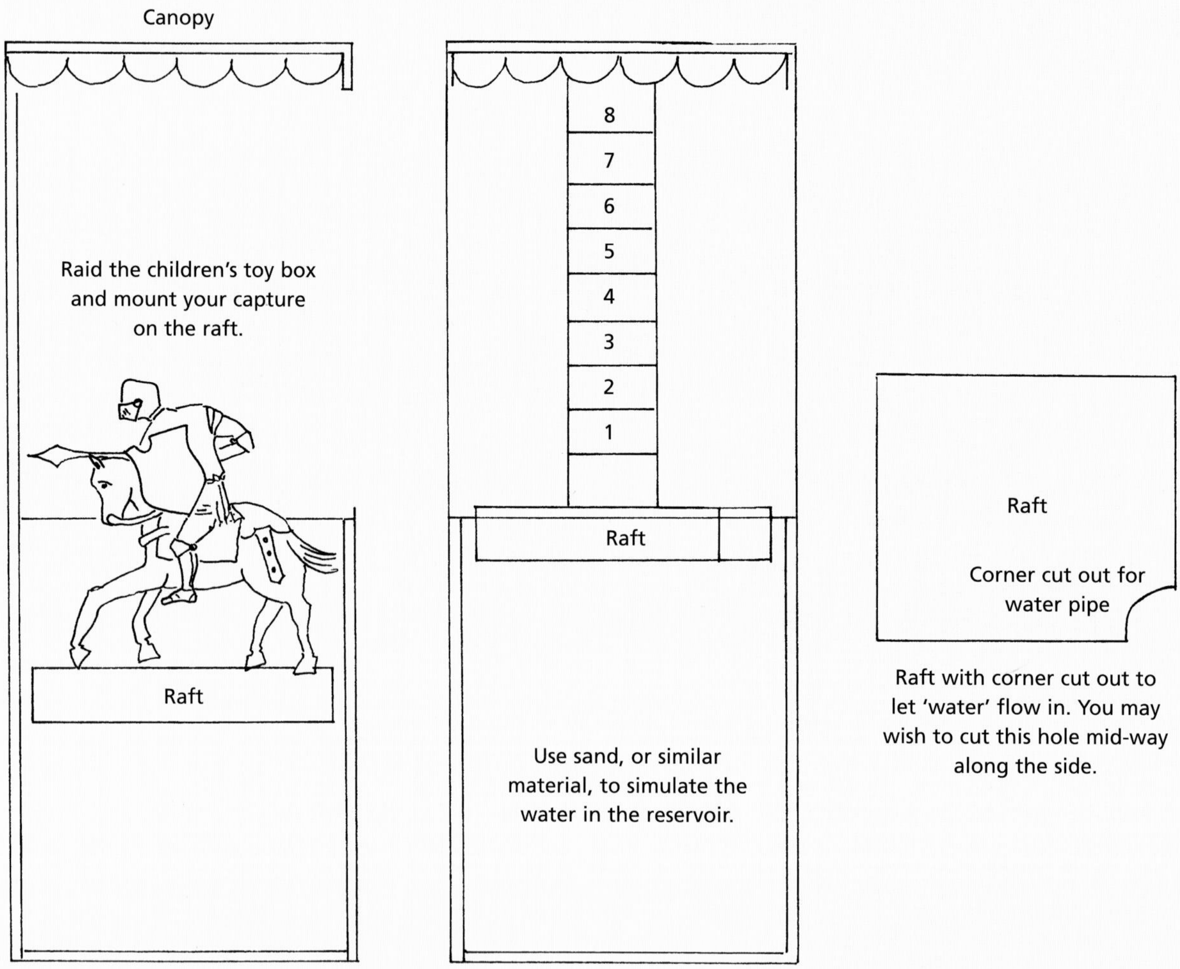

Canopy

Raid the children's toy box and mount your capture on the raft.

Raft

8
7
6
5
4
3
2
1

Raft

Use sand, or similar material, to simulate the water in the reservoir.

Raft

Corner cut out for water pipe

Raft with corner cut out to let 'water' flow in. You may wish to cut this hole mid-way along the side.

N.B. DIAGRAMS ARE ACTUAL SIZE

Make the back board with the hours on it only a little higher than the depth of the reservoir, to allow for the decoration and canopy.

Mount your figure on a platform, to simulate a raft, and position your 'raft' in the box, so that it appears to be floating on water in the reservoir.

Sit your 'pointer' on the raft, indicating 'zero' – that is, the lowest position.

To be authentic decorate the model using flat/matt paints in reds, green, white and old gold, and it will then brighten up a dark corner in your dolls' house.

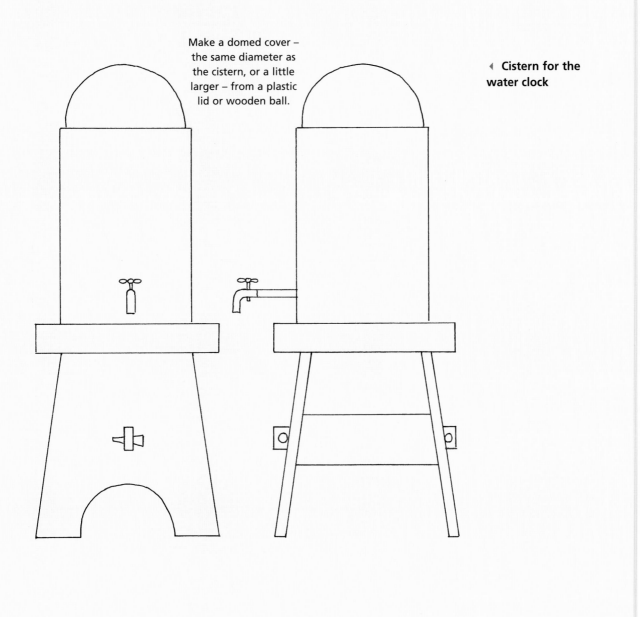

Make a domed cover – the same diameter as the cistern, or a little larger – from a plastic lid or wooden ball.

◄ **Cistern for the water clock**

MUSICAL INSTRUMENTS

In our period England was known as Merry England. Music was an important part of life, and most people were able to play a pleasing tune with even the simplest of instruments.

A strange stringed instrument still used today, and again depicted in church carvings and paintings, is the hurdy-gurdy (see below). Like the pipes, it had drones in the form of stopped-off strings vibrated by a hand-cranked wheel, and keys to give the tune being played by the left hand. This instrument was mainly a toy of the rich, but today it is one of the most prevalent instruments used by European folk groups.

The psaltery was quite sweet while the racket and shawm were well-named. In between these were the bladders and pipes and the crumhorn (see page 178). All of these can be made using wire and spindles with a lot of polish to finish off.

Today the main church instrument is the organ.

▲ A friction drum, 1629

This drawing is after a painting by Jan Molenaer in the National Gallery, London. It shows a boy playing a friction drum, a simple home-made instrument made from a large earthenware pot, with a soft piece of leather or skin pulled tight over the top. This was held in place by a leather thong or stout home-made twine. The skin was pierced by a long smooth stick, which was deftly moved up and down to give a tune.

▼ Hurdy gurdy

This belonged to Adelaide, third daughter of Louis XV.

BAGPIPES

▲ Simple as they were, there are many variations on the bagpipes. This drawing of an unshaven peasant playing this ancient instrument, is a detail from *Peasant Dance*, a painting by Pieter Brueghel the Elder (1520–69), who painted many peasants playing musical instruments. This set has a chanter to give the melody and two long drones over the shoulder for harmony.

▲ Some variations of the pipes can be found in church carvings and on tombstones, and I show three here: one is on the end of a church bench and shows pipes with one drone and one chanter; another is a misericord at Beverley Minster, Yorkshire, showing a monkey 'playing' a dog, while the third is in the same county at Ripon, and shows a pig playing pipes of one drone and a chanter.

◀ **Traditional bellows-type bagpipes**

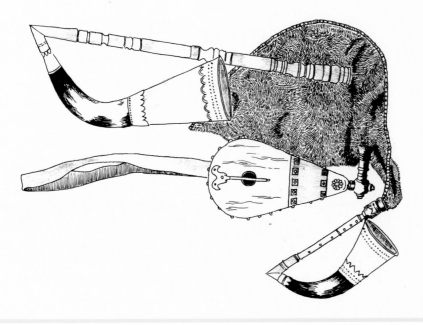

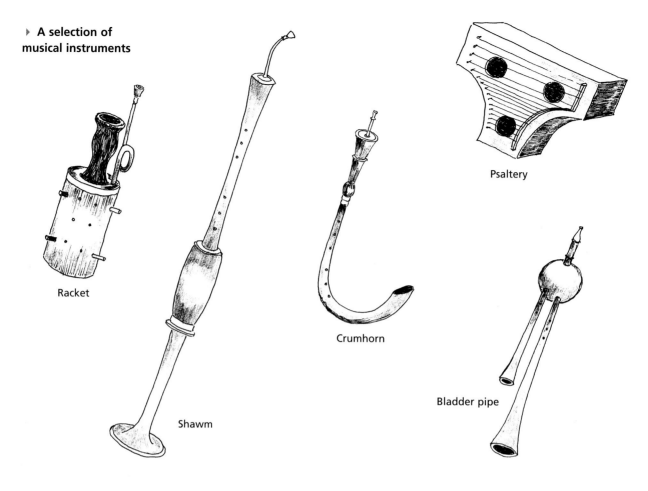

Racket

Shawm

Crumhorn

Psaltery

Bladder pipe

Angels can be found playing hand-held versions in many a church and two versions are shown on the facing page, one pre-Tudor and one early Tudor. They were held on the knee and had a bellows at the back and buttons to allow air up the pipes. This is a clever little instrument and not beyond most miniaturists' competence, even if it will not play.

Virginals got their name because they were the instrument favoured by nuns. Henry VIII had 35 clavichordia virginale *'made harp fashion of cipres with keies of ivorie'*. Not all were set up like mini grand pianos but some, like the organ, were set up on end as if they knew we miniaturists were short of space, and known as the 'clavicytherium' (see illustration, right). Most musical instruments, however, were of the peasant variety and the differing names given to the same instrument were also vernacular. So fill your house with music – even the trombone falls into our period.

▲ **Clavicytherium**

ORGANS

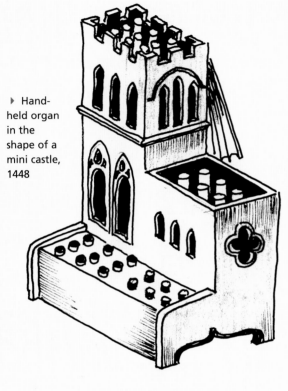

▶ Hand-held organ in the shape of a mini castle, 1448

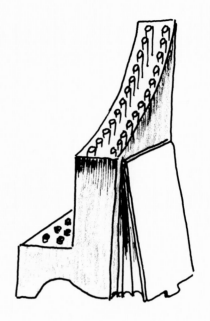

▲ Late fifteenth-century hand-held organ

The two hand-held organs above have bellows at the back, and were played by buttons, not keys.

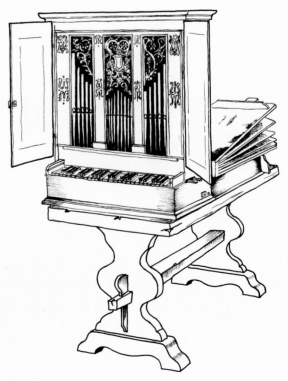

▶ Sixteenth-century positive organ resting on an attractive period table. The table most of us could make, even the bellows at a push, and all that is left to do is make a cupboard and fill it with pipes. Various rich woods were used, but we can buy the plastic ones, so use those.

CHAPTER ELEVEN

CREATURES GREAT AND SMALL

Dovecotes • Kennels • Pigsties • Beehives • Mousetraps

They had neither refrigerator nor ice house, so food had to be smoked, salted, dried, pickled, set in jellies or better still kept fresh, whether in the fish pond, conyger (rabbit warren), or dovecote, that sure sign of a gentleman's house.

Pigeons, like swans, pair for life and will live peaceably with large numbers of their own kind. In a dry, warm and secure dovecote they will breed freely, the hen producing two eggs every six or seven weeks, and continuing in this way for most of the year. The pair would feed and fatten the resulting fledgling or squabs, which in turn were harvested for the kitchen of the big house. People may have tired of it but it was fresh and on hand, and cost little to harvest.

DOVECOTES

At first dovecotes were a symbol of manorial privilege and jealously guarded by their owners, whether parson or bishop. As a status symbol they were freestanding and distinctive, being quite tall, and with at least five hundred nesting holes.

Nesting holes were reached by an ingenious device known as a 'potence', which was simply a pair of arms attached to the top of a central vertical shaft which rotated as required. Ladders were fixed just short of the ends of the arms so that they hung from top to bottom some 6–8in (15.2–20cm) from the wall, thus allowing eggs and squabs to be taken.

▲ **Little Moreton Hall, Cheshire, England**
Dovecote in gable or service wing.

◄ ▲ **A simple, round structure lined with nest holes**
This still retains its potence. Unlike most dovecotes, it has no ledges in front of the nest holes (see facing page) so, to make up for it, there are two feeding platforms attached to the central post of the potence.

A good example of a potence still hangs in the Priory Dovecote, Dunster, Somerset.

In northern France they made a good stab at timber-framed dovecotes, building many-sided ones, some being just short of circular (see overleaf).

English timber-framed dovecotes were rectangular and, as a rule, box-framed. But at least one small cruck-framed one exists, which was built for the use of a local clergyman at Glebe Farm, Hill Croome, Worcestershire. The nesting holes in most timber-framed structures were of wattle and daub and they survive in a dovecote at Long Wittenham Manor, Oxfordshire.

One problem with rectangular dovecotes was that the potence could not reach the nest holes in the corners, so a system of walkways and steps or ladders had to be used. Perhaps the best known one is that at Luntley Court, Herefordshire.

Crèuecoeur   Caudemone   Les Tourelles

▲ **Timber-framed French dovecotes**

▲ **Section of a model dovecote**

This shows the row upon row of nest boxes, each with a ledge in front. To collect the young birds, you had to use the 'potence', which, with its ladder, rotated as required. Many variations of dovecote still exist, and make good projects.

▲ **Dovecote, Luntley Court, Hereford, England**

KENNELS

Dogs were used in great numbers for herding sheep and cows, bull-baiting and hunting, but we will look at a more domestic creature, the guard dog, which was housed close to the entrance of a house. In my demonstration model of a panel-framed house (see page 21) I put a kennel in the thickness of the outside wall of a large brick chimney, but it could be tucked into any void, be it under the stairs or in a buttress. The choice is yours, depending on the shape of your house and a suitable void being found, but a few doves and a dog would bring a little something to your dolls' house.

▼ **Little Moreton Hall, Congleton, Cheshire**
This dog kennel is just in the courtyard, formed by a gap in the wattle and daub infill in the timber wall. Note the iron ring on the right, and the stone trough in front. The block of wood forms a half-door, and can be removed for cleaning.

Circular pigsty

PIGSTIES

A number of pigsties have been re-erected at the Museum of Welsh Life, at St Fagans, Cardiff, including this circular one (left) which has a domed construction. They are of ancient heritage, with the same method of construction being used for human dwellings throughout Europe. Not only pigs but hens, geese and ducks were housed in smaller versions, keeping an ancient tradition active well into the nineteenth century.

BEEHIVES

There were many variations in the way hives were made, but one thought to be an Irish variant is now known to have been used in southern England as well as Antrim, Ireland. This was made from reeds, rushes or long straw, and had a conical cover or hood. It was mounted on a wooden platform part way up a stout but short post, to keep it out of contact with the cold, damp ground.

There are ceramic hives on the miniatures market, but you could make them yourself using polymer clay. I have made miniatures using rough garden twine and a wooden form which can be removed.

How an 'Irish' beehive was made

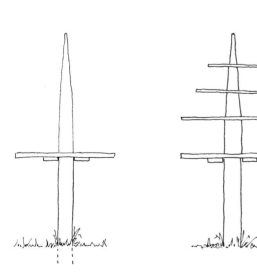

1 Post and wooden platform

2 With frame for cover and combs added

3 Completed hive. Cover can be made using coconut fibre. First a frame of hazel rods was attached to the post to which a wooden platform had been secured. The cap of straw, rush or reed was positioned over this and the top tied to the post with the rushes, and so on, being held in place by hoops of wood, metal or rope. The English version was of willow, hazel and/or straw. While we tend to think of the flight hole for the bees being in the bottom of the hive, old drawings show them being anything up to three-quarters of the way up.

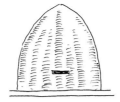

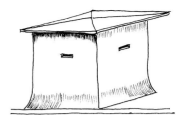

| Fourteenth century | Mid-fifteenth century | 1531 | Mid-fifteenth century |

▲ Beehives

Examples from period illustrations. While most beehives were woven, some were of wood. The position of the flight holes varies according to region.

▲ Beehives in a simple rustic shelter

The ancient type, at the Museum of Welsh Life at St Fagans, Cardiff. There are many period illustrations of hives just like these in similar shelters of stone or wood. They are made from coiled straw rope and are simple to replicate in miniature.

◀ Cottage beehives of straw

This is protected by an old sack and a large terracotta pot.

MOUSETRAPS

The mouse has shared our home for centuries and its presence has been recorded in many ways.

One early depiction is to be found in a painting of 1425 showing St Joseph with a mousetrap of the drop-weight type which has been in use for over 500 years. A version is shown below.

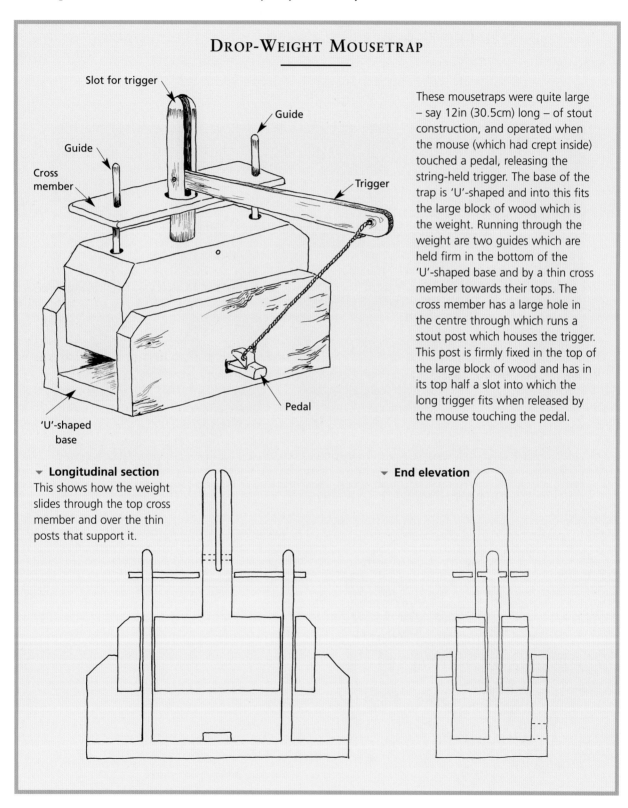

DROP-WEIGHT MOUSETRAP

Slot for trigger

Guide

Guide

Cross member

Trigger

Pedal

'U'-shaped base

These mousetraps were quite large – say 12in (30.5cm) long – of stout construction, and operated when the mouse (which had crept inside) touched a pedal, releasing the string-held trigger. The base of the trap is 'U'-shaped and into this fits the large block of wood which is the weight. Running through the weight are two guides which are held firm in the bottom of the 'U'-shaped base and by a thin cross member towards their tops. The cross member has a large hole in the centre through which runs a stout post which houses the trigger. This post is firmly fixed in the top of the large block of wood and has in its top half a slot into which the long trigger fits when released by the mouse touching the pedal.

▼ Longitudinal section
This shows how the weight slides through the top cross member and over the thin posts that support it.

▼ End elevation

CHAPTER TWELVE

AND SO TO BED

Beds and Bed Construction • Warming the Bed • Cradles

BEDS AND BED CONSTRUCTION

Beds were of great importance and, for most people, the most expensive item in the house. You were conceived in one, born in one and hoped to die in one, and in your will left your best one to your first-born. There were special beds known as birthing beds, there were beds like the Great Bed of Ware (see page 190) and there were gun or sabre beds, and we will look at how to make them.

▼ **Models of great beds, c. 1560–1610**

GREAT BEDS

Great beds are large and richly decorated tester beds (i.e. with canopies), which were found in great houses. Most importantly, the ornate legs or posts which hold up the fine tester are not attached to the bed frame.

Today we refer to great beds as four-posters, but originally they only had two posts, the tester or roof resting on the large headboard at one end and on two posts at the other end. Other variations had both ends of the tester supported by a panelled board, and some early beds had no posts at the foot, with the tester being hung from ceiling beams and resting on the headboard, which was known then as a 'dosser'.

PROJECT
MAKE A GREAT BED

1 Start at the bottom by constructing a dais ½in high x 6in wide x at least 7½in long (1.2 x 15.2 x 19cm).

2 Build the bed base, 1½in high x 4in wide x 5½in long (3.8 x 10.1 x 14cm), on top of the dais.

3 Make a headboard, 6in (15.2cm) high, and fix it to the top end of the bed base. You can decorate this as much as you wish, as most Tudor beds were not the dark oak we are used to today, but were painted bright colours.

4 The legs should be 6in (15.2cm) high and the turned section – the post – 3in (7.5cm) high. The base is where you have fun as these are on display at all times, with any curtains you may hang being inside them. My drawing shows three variations: the one with four columns in the base is modelled on the Great Bed of Ware.

▼ **Great bed legs**
Legs on great beds are detached from the bed frame, and come in many shapes. Some – like the one shown on the left below – were made to hold a chamber pot.

Great beds were the norm if you were rich, and the super-rich or lucky had feathers and down to rest on. It was thought healthy for the gentry to sleep almost in a sitting position, but the labourer was too tired for this and stretched out.

Generally the poor slept on a hurdle or a woven straw mattress on the floor, with a covering of rough cloth or skins, but a lucky few, who were a little better off, would have used it on a half-headed bed.

This looked rather like a modern bed, but was much less comfortable. It had a low headboard and may have had a footboard, and there were many ways of supporting the mattress, or whatever you had in lieu of one.

More comfortable was a bag of heather, straw or chaff and John Evelyn, the English author, recommended freshly fallen beech leaves gathered about the fall, before they were frost-damaged.

General Bed Construction

The following diagrams show how boards, planks and ropes were attached to the bed frame. Boards could cover the whole bed, or be 6in (15.2cm) wide and set at 6in (15.2cm) intervals. The holes for ropes to pass through, and the pegs ropes passed around, were also set at 6in (15.2cm) intervals.

The ends of the ropes were held by a wooden pin, hammered into the hole with the rope end in it. When the ropes required adjustment the pin was removed, the rope tightened, the pin replaced and you 'slept tight'. I am sure there are many ways of doing this, but below are the ones I have recorded.

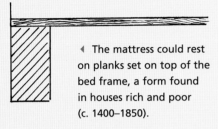

◀ The mattress could rest on planks set on top of the bed frame, a form found in houses rich and poor (c. 1400–1850).

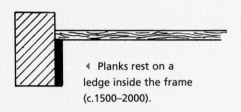

◀ Planks rest on a ledge inside the frame (c.1500–2000).

◀ Holes were drilled through all four sides of the frame, then rope passed through the holes and interwoven, to form a net or mesh on which to rest the mattress (c. 1525–1850).

◀ The frame was given a groove that ran round all four sides and the holes drilled in the groove. Now when the rope is threaded through it is recessed in the groove (c. 1550–1850).

◀ A groove was cut into the upper face of the frame and the holes drilled downwards at an angle, so that they came out midway down the inner face of the frame (c. 1560–1850).

▲ Holes were drilled into the upper face of the frame but not through it. Into these holes wooden pegs were inserted so that they protruded some 2in (5cm) above the frame. The mesh of rope was then woven around the pegs (1600–1850).

▲ A slightly more complicated variation: the frame is built with all four sides at an angle, sloping in towards the top. Holes are then drilled in the underside, the pegs inserted and the ropes woven round them. This allowed the mattress to sink down inside the frame (1625–1850).

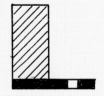

▲ The bottom edge of the frame had a plank or strip of wood fitted to the underside, which projected 3in (7.5cm) in towards the middle of the bed. Holes were drilled in this, then the ropes woven as previously (c. 1625–1850).

THE GREAT BED OF WARE

This renowned Tudor bed is richly decorated with fine carving and inlay and is – for the most part – painted, as was most woodwork of the time. At 11ft 1in long x 10ft 8½in wide x 8ft high (approximately 3.38 x 3. 26 x 2.44m) – about twice the size of most great beds of the period – it housed as many people as could get into it. Its fame is that, while it resided in the Saracen's Head inn in the town of Ware, England, eight butchers and their wives slept in it all together. It may, originally, have been built for a house, but this was just how you would have been lodged in a sixteenth-century inn.

Dates given for the construction of this bed range from 1463 to 1570, but we know that it was in the Saracen's Head until the nineteenth century, then moved to Rye House in Sussex and later to its present home, the Victoria and Albert Museum, in London.

In 1601, when Shakespeare wrote *Twelfth Night*, Sir Andrew Aguecheek remembers the bed when he remarks '*as many lies as will lie in thy sheet of paper, although the sheet were big enough for the Bed of Ware*'.

BURTHEN PINS

Some people go to bed, fall asleep and never move. Others toss and turn, throwing off the blankets. In Tudor times they came up with a simple solution, so that many beds of the late Tudor or early Jacobean period have three holes in the top of the frame towards the top of the bed. These strange holes once held everything in place.

Reconstructions I have seen are about 18in (46cm) long and can be simple round sticks, known as 'burthen pins', or richly carved, or turned pins. Period illustrations show that when the bed was a death bed, candles were mounted on top of the pins. If and when greater comfort was required, the ropes forming the mesh were tightened, with your servant who had just completed the task saying 'Good night, sleep tight'.

Randle Holme (1627–99) was a painter of heraldry who attempted to prove lines between everyday things and their heraldic interpretations, no matter how contrived, but at least recorded them showing us their use:

▸ **Burthen pin (c. 1450–1650)**

'*Things usefull about a bed, and bed-chamber. Bed stocks, as Bed posts, sides, ends, Head and Tester.*
Mat, or sack-cloth Bottom
Cord, Bed staves, and stay or the feet.
Curtain Rods and hookes, and rings, either brass or horn.
Beds, of chaffe, Wool or flocks, Feathers, and down in Ticks or Bed Tic.
Bolsters, pillows.
Blankets, Ruggs, Quilts, Counterpan, caddows.
Curtaines, Valens, Tester head cloth; all either fringed, laced or plaine alike.
Inner curtains and Valens, which are generally White silk or Linen.
Tester Bobbs of Wood gilt or covered suitable to the curtaines.
Tester top either flat, or Raised, or canopy like, or half Testered.
Basis, or the lower Valens at the seat of the Bed, which reacheth to the ground, and fringed for state as the upper Valens, either with Inch fring, caul fring, Tufted fring, snailing fring, Gimpe fring with tufts and Buttons, Vellem fring, Ec.'

▲ **Carcass of a truckle bed, which hasn't yet been strung**
A truckle bed would slide under another bed and be brought out for use by a personal servant.

Randle Holme's date of birth makes this information relevant to Jacobean and later Stuart beds, but bear in mind that the beds he describes are not for farm workers and the like, but for gentlefolk. He went on to write about more humble furniture:

'*as a Bed with blankett or Cadow or Rugg; or covering: the sheets turned down, and a boulster … this is a bed prepared for to*

lodge in, but with no tester. Such are termed Truckle beds, because they troundle under other beds: or being made higher with an head, so that they may be set in a chamber corner, or under a cant roofe they are called field bed or cant bed. If it be so, that it may have a canapy over it (that is a half tester) then it is termed a canapy bed: to which bed belongs curtaines and Vellance.'

▼ **The Burthen Staffe**
The small drawing is based on No. 81 in *The Randle Holme Heraldic Interpretations of Everyday Things*. This is his simple bed, of which he wrote: '*in the base of this square lys a bed staffe, of some termed a burthen staffe*'.

▼ **Amorous couple on a truckle bed**
This drawing shows an amorous couple seated on a truckle bed, with a burthen pin holding the bedclothes of the main bed back. This is the only representation I know that shows such a pin at the foot of the bed.

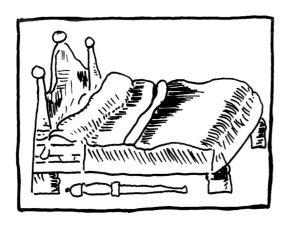

BIRTHING BEDS

Birthing beds, which consisted of a bed set on a dais or steps, as if ready for an adoration, were made in most parts of Europe around 1350–1550.

Under the bed there were a number of drawers, almost unknown in Tudor England in any furniture, indicating that these were used by the super-rich only. Usually, there were no posts at the foot of the bed, so the tester was slung from the ceiling.

PROJECT
MAKE A BIRTHING BED

This single bed has an ornate headboard, and side curtains are hung on metal rods hinged on the headboard. Under the bed there is a row of drawers either side, and it sits on a dais.

The dais can be made longer than the bed, as shown here, giving a step on all three sides. There is no tester but a fabric one can be hung overhead as in the period illustrations.

1 Build the dais 5in (12.7cm) wide by 6½in (16.5cm) long and ¾in (19mm) high.

2 Construct the base of the bed, 3in (7.5cm) wide by 5½in (14cm) long, with 1in (2.5cm) square-fronted drawers along each side. When complete, attach to the dais.

3 Build the headboard 5in (12.7cm) above the bed, or to a height suitable for your room, then fix the curtain rods and, when the unit is complete, glue it in position.

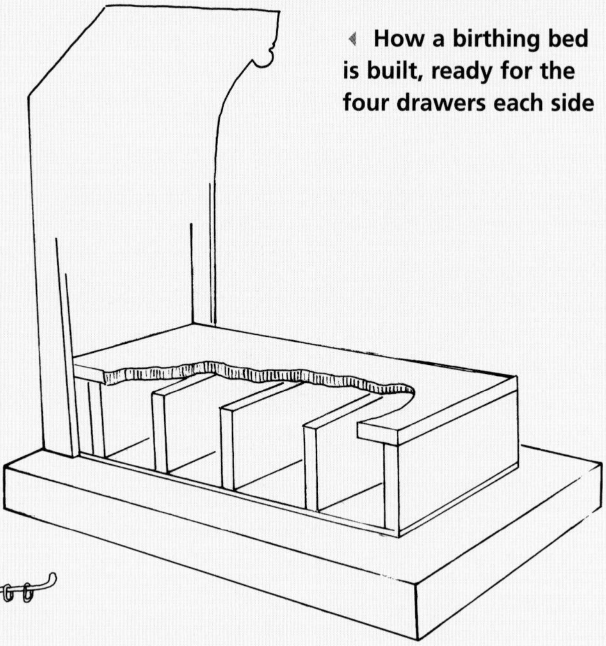

◀ **How a birthing bed is built, ready for the four drawers each side**

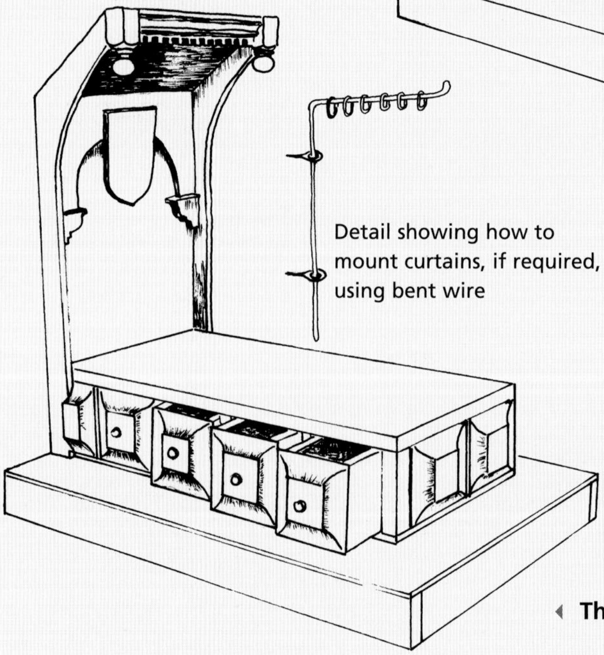

Detail showing how to mount curtains, if required, using bent wire

Headboard

◀ **The completed birthing bed**

GUN BED, c. 1550–1650

The gun bed, which is still to be found in some old houses, is a thing of legend. A gun or sabre was kept in a box built into the foot of the bed and a Bible was kept in a special cupboard built into the head. It is said that intruders were despatched at one end of the bed, had a small biblical quotation read over them at the other end, and the purveyor of justice could then have a conscience-free night. Such beds date from c. 1550 to 1650. All the examples I know of have fielded panels, rather the richer linenfold ones, which were going out of fashion at this time. (See project overleaf.)

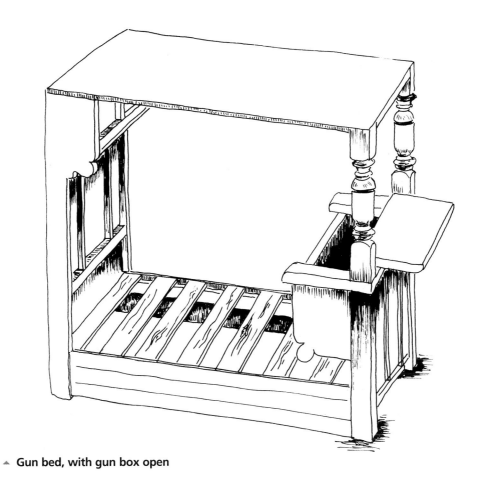

▲ **Gun bed, with gun box open**

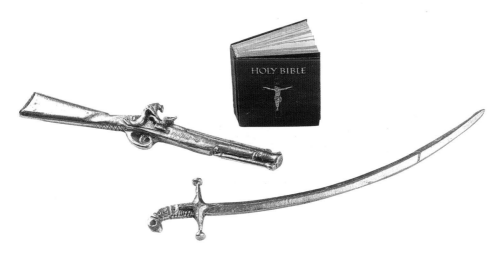

PROJECT
MAKE A GUN BED

This bed looks complicated but, if taken step by step, it is achievable. It consists of base, foot with built-in gun box, headboard with Bible box, and tester. The dimensions are: 6in high x 4in wide x 6in long (15.2 x 10.1 x 15.2cm).

1 Build the box-like base 6in long x 4in wide x 1½in high (15.2 x 10.1 x 3.8cm). The top can be one piece of wood or it can be slatted using ½in (12mm) wide material. You could decorate the sides using panels, if you wish.

2 Construct the gun box and foot of the bed. As the posts I use are 3in (7.5cm) high the footboard and its gun box must also be 3in (7.5cm) high to give us that important 6in (15.2cm) height. The lid of the box can be hinged using small brass hinges to be painted black, or pins can be pushed through either side of the frame. The outer face has three fielded panels glued on it.

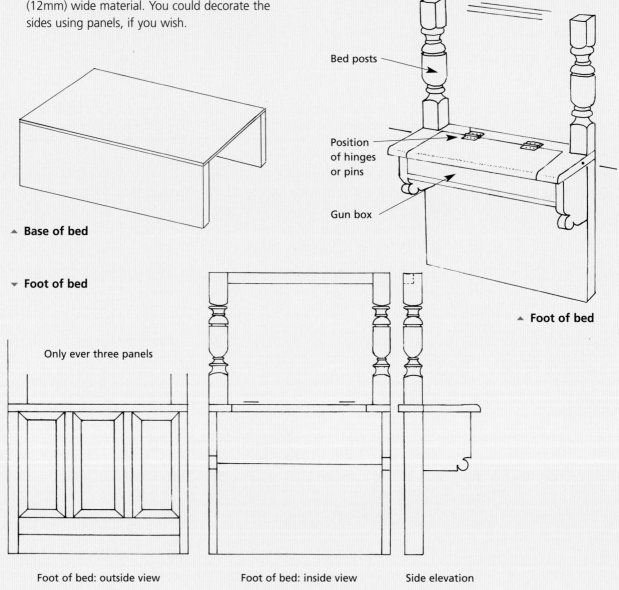

▲ Base of bed

▼ Foot of bed

Bed posts

Position of hinges or pins

Gun box

▲ Foot of bed

Only ever three panels

Foot of bed: outside view

Foot of bed: inside view

Side elevation

Open space at top to receive the Bible box

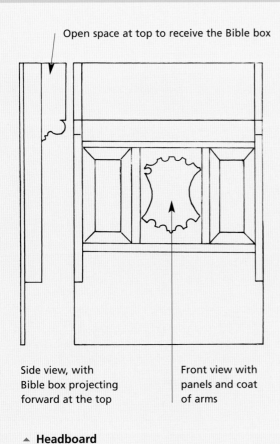

Side view, with
Bible box projecting
forward at the top

Front view with
panels and coat
of arms

▲ **Headboard**

3 The headboard is 6in (15.2cm) high
and 4in (10.1cm) wide and can be highly
decorated. The choice is yours. Any
decoration must take into consideration
the 1½in (3.8cm) high base and the Bible
box, which can be built in isolation then
mounted in position when complete.

4 Fit Bible box first, followed by undecorated
tester. The decoration is applied last. For
the tester use thin wood about ⅟₁₆in (2mm)
thick on the underside panels. It is best to
fix the tester and its frame or edging prior
to fitting the panels.

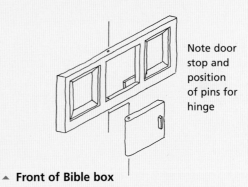

Note door
stop and
position
of pins for
hinge

▲ **Front of Bible box**

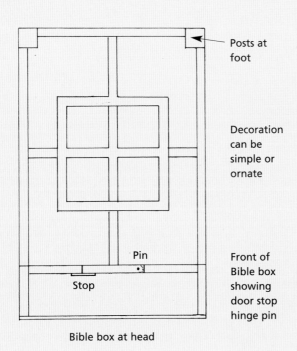

Posts at
foot

Decoration
can be
simple or
ornate

Pin

Stop

Front of
Bible box
showing
door stop
hinge pin

Bible box at head

▲ **Underside of tester**

WARMING THE BED

BED WARMERS

Most people like to climb into a warm bed on a cold winter's night and you are fortunate if your partner has warmed it up for you. This is following an ancient custom, as there was a time when a master had a servant climb in some time prior to his going to bed, so that it was warmed through and suitable for a gentleman of quality. The modern term 'bed warmer' is derived from that simple act.

There are many references to bed warmers other than human ones, but just what sort of machine they were we do not know. What we do know is that the bed warmer so beloved of miniaturists, which looks like a long-handled frying pan, did not come into use until just after the Tudor period. You can, with an engraving tool or a fine drill, customize one of the many examples available, but do remember they are Stuart, Jacobean, not Tudor.

The wooden handles we know today, which are usually on this type of warming pan, are late seventeenth century to Georgian. Early ones had metal handles, be they iron or steel, with bowls or pans of brass, copper or silver.

▲ **A marriage token or gift?**
This bed warmer, which is in the Victoria and Albert Museum, London, is 47in (113cm) long. The lid is finely engraved and pierced, showing a couple in mid-seventeenth-century costume with peacocks and flowers.

▲ **The earliest known brass warming pan, 1615**
This has a handle 42in (106cm) long and a brass pan 10in (25.5cm) in diameter. The lid is engraved with the Arms of the Earl of Essex, and shows his crest of a reindeer with a coronet for a collar and as some form of restraint. An inscription round the rim is as follows: 'The: Right: Hon: The: Earle: of: Essix: His: Armes', and it sits on a row of small pierced holes.

HISTORICAL REFERENCE

The Earl of Essex, mentioned left, was the son of Robert Devereux, the Earl of Essex who was beheaded when he ran foul of Elizabeth I. Prior to this he had been a prominent figure in Elizabethan society, and was one of the heroes of Cadiz when in 1596 he, along with Raleigh, set about burning the ships of the Spanish fleet in the harbour there. He was also sent to Ireland, to subdue the locals. However, he came home early, having had little military success, formed a group with others to plot against the Queen, and so lost his head.

BED WAGONS

The bed wagon, or bed car, had wooden frames to hold the blankets up and allow the heat from a pan of ashes to permeate the area. The pan sat on a trivet in a metal tray held in the wooden frame. Above these, held in the top frame, was another metal tray to protect the blankets directly over the hot ashes. If your house is Tudor or Stewart, you should have this machine rather than the more elegant frying-pan type. If your house is Stuart/Jacobean, then you can have either, as the bed wagon was still in use in the Victorian era.

PROJECT

MAKE A BED WAGON

1 Cut four lengths of ³⁄₁₆in (4mm) square wood, 3–5in (7.5–12.7cm) long, depending on the size of the bed that the wagon is to be used on.

2 Paint some cocktail sticks, to represent the metal rods that were used as spacers.

3 Drill the four lengths of wood and glue the spacers in place. To ensure everything is even, push the frame up tight against blocks of wood until the glue on the spacers is set.

4 Cut strips of thin plywood, ³⁄₁₆in (4mm) wide, to represent the thin metal hoops that hold the blankets, but take care, as the plywood is fragile.

5 Glue the hoops in place, allowing large overlaps.

6 Cut the two small metal trays out of alloy cans or strips of fine plywood (if you use alloy cans, file or sand the sides down, as they are sharp). Charcoal could be held in any container that sat on the bottom tray.

7 Secure the metal trays in place on the inside of the frame with fine wire.

8 Paint all 'metal' parts, but leave the wooden frame plain, taking on the patina of use and age.

9 Add a metal trivet, and a small container for the charcoal used as fuel to complete the bed wagon.

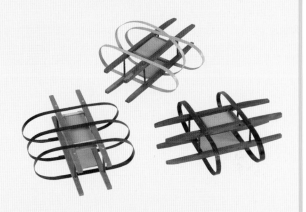

▲ **Model bed wagons**

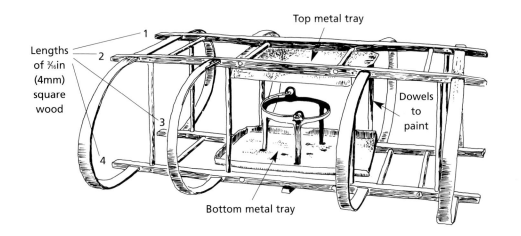

Top metal tray

Lengths of ³⁄₁₆in (4mm) square wood

1
2
3
4

Dowels to paint

Bottom metal tray

◀ **A 3ft (1m) long bed wagon**
This bed wagon was mentioned by the landscape gardener Gertrude Jekyll, who worked on gardens with architect Sir Edwin Lutyens.

CRADLES

Cradles for most families were straw or wicker baskets without rockers which, when soiled beyond redemption, would be used as fuel for the oven. Some were supported on a wooden frame to bring them up to the same height as the parents' bed, while a lucky few would even have had rockers, but they were not regarded as essential.

Cradles of wood came in many shapes, with some rocking from end to end and others from side to side. My observations show that those in central Europe rocked from side to side, while in Scandinavia and by the Mediterranean they rocked from end to end. Rocking posts were an early refinement and could protrude 3–12in (7.5–30.5cm) above the end of a cradle. Later, the end and part of the sides were made higher, to keep draughts off the child's head, then a hinged hood was introduced, and later still this was fixed.

Rockers extended beyond the sides of cradles to prevent overturning, but were also used to rock the cradle with a foot. Early rockers were at the ends and attached to the corner or rocking posts, while later ones were fixed to the floor of the cradle, then, after some time, moved in 4 or 5in (10.1–12.7cm) from the ends.

Early cradles did not have a hood, but most had a series of holes, hoops, buckles or knobs in their sides to which the tails of the swaddling bands were secured. The bottoms of many cradles were not simply one large plank, but could be made up of spaced lathes, and many were even strung like the best of period beds.

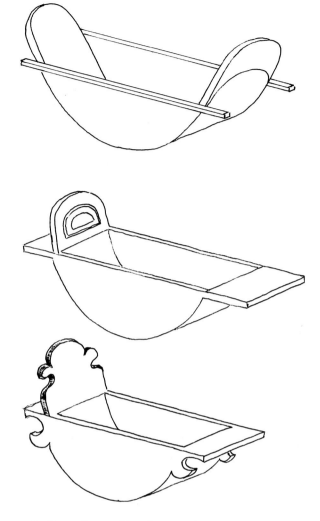

▲ **Early cradles rocking from end to end**
Some nineteenth-century north-European cradles are mounted on rockers which run from end to end, looking a bit like a sleigh.

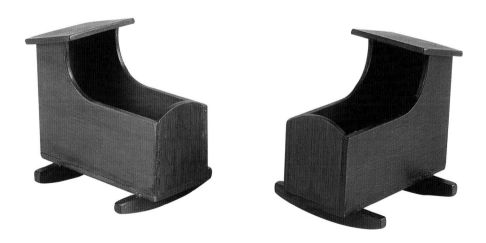

▸ **Model cradles, with canopies**
These were used c. 1620 onwards.

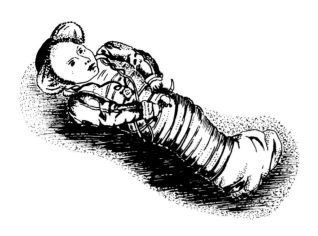

▲ Baby in swaddling, 1581
The tails of the swaddling bands were tied to the knobs and so on, at the top edge of the cradle.

▲ Late fifteenth-century cradle
This hangs from a pair of upright posts on trestle feet with carved Gothic brackets, and was originally painted and gilded. Legend says it was used by the baby Henry V who was born in 1388, but the cradle dates from c. 1500.

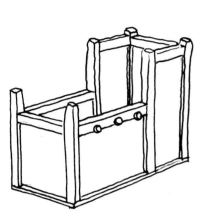

▲ Cradle of 1549
This cradle has no rockers, but has knobs for the swaddling bands.

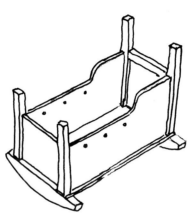

▲ Cradle of 1550
This cradle has rockers at the ends and holes for the tails of the swaddling bands.

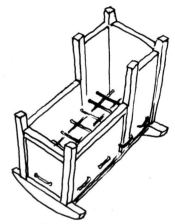

▲ Cradle of 1560
This cradle has rockers at the ends, but now there are ropes in the base, like beds of the period.

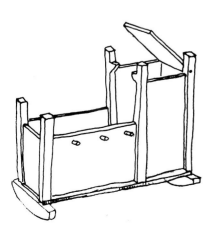

◀ Cradle of 1650
A hinged hood has been introduced, and pegs for the swaddling bands.

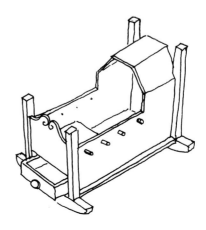

◀ Cradle of 1656
Pegs for swaddling bands and a drawer for a hot brick are featured here. The hood may be later.

▲ This cradle belonged to Anne of Denmark
Anne of Denmark was the wife of James VI of Scotland and I of England, and mother of Charles I.

▼ Model of a child's bed
This child would have had parents of some standing.

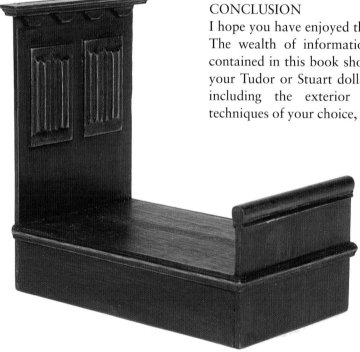

High cradles supported by upright posts could be kept within the curtains of a bed to keep the baby warm and allow the mother to rock it in the night. It was not unusual for the wealthy parent to provide two cradles, one for show and one for use. The one for show was known as the 'cradle of estate' and had rich ornament and layers of blankets and quilts – not always a good thing. Tragic consequences were recorded in the case of Richard, son of Evely, who died at the tender age of five years and three days. An entry in a diary records that his son was

> ' ... *suffocated by ye women and maids that tended him and covered him too hot with blankets as he lay in a cradle near a hot fire in a closed room.*'

Blankets and bedclothes could be rich in the extreme: Margaret of Flanders, the aunt of Edward IV had a furrier garnish a cradle with the skins of 1,200 ermine. Lower down the social scale it was traditional to line a cradle with sphagnum moss, so as to absorb certain fluids that from time to time escaped from the baby. At the end of the week, required or not, the moss was cleaned out. The use of moss gave us the traditional shade of green used to paint the inside of most cradles up until the nineteenth century. In some areas where reindeer moss was used, the paint was a dusty blue.

CONCLUSION
I hope you have enjoyed this journey back in time. The wealth of information and historical detail contained in this book should enable you to make your Tudor or Stuart dolls' house truly authentic, including the exterior and interior building techniques of your choice, and suitable furnishings.

BIBLIOGRAPHY

HISTORICAL BACKGROUND

Milton, Giles
*Big Chief Elizabeth: How England's
Adventurers Gambled and Won the
New World*
Hodder & Stoughton, 2000
ISBN: 0340748818

Ridley, Jasper
A Brief History of the Tudor Age
Robinson, 2002
ISBN: 1841194719

ARCHITECTURE

Cooper, Nicholas
Houses of the Gentry, 1480–1680
Published for The Paul Mellon
Centre for Studies in British Art in
Association with English Heritage
Yale University Press, 1999
ISBN: 0300073909

Faucon & Lescroart
Manor Houses in Normandy
Könemann, 1995
ISBN: 3895087033

Garrett, Wendell
American Colonial
Taschen, 1995
ISBN: 382288278X

Hilling, J. B.
The Historical Architecture of Wales
The University of Wales, 1975
ISBN: 0708306268

Howe, J. W.
American House
Batsford, 2000
ISBN: 0713487968

Lloyd, Nathaniel
*A History of the English House
from Primitive Times to the
Victorian Period*
Architectural Press, 1975
ISBN 0851392865
and
A History of English Brickwork
Antique Collectors' Club, 1983
ISBN: 0907462367

McKean, Charles
*The Scottish Chateau: the Country
House of Renaissance Scotland*
Sutton, 2004
ISBN: 0750935278

Taylor, Alec Clifton
The Pattern of English Building
Faber, 1987
ISBN: 0571139884

Wood, Margaret
The English Medieval House
Phoenix, 1965
ISBN: 460078135

FIXTURES AND FITTINGS

Alcock & Hall
*Fixtures and Fittings in Dated
Houses, 1567–1763*
Council for British
Archaeology, 1994
ISBN: 1872414524

Calloway, Stephen
*The Elements of Style: an
Encyclopedia of Domestic
Architectural Detail*
Mitchell Beazley, 1996
ISBN: 1857328345

Roberts, Hugh D.
Down Hearth to Bar Grate
Wiltshire Life Folk Society, 1981
ISBN: 090775600X

FURNISHING

Chinnery, Victor
Oak Furniture – The British Tradition
Antique Collectors' Club, 1979
ISBN: 0902028618

Edwards, Ralph
The Dictionary of English Furniture
Antique Collectors' Club
ISBN: 185149345X

Evans, E. Estyn
Irish Folk Ways
Routledge, 1988
ISBN: 0415002257

Hurrell, J. Weymouth
*Measured Drawings of Old Oak
English Furniture*
B. T. Batsford, 1902

Kevill-Davies, Sally
Yesterday's Children
Antique Collectors' Club, 1991
ISBN: 1851491848

Yarwood, Doreen
The English Home
B. T. Batsford, 1956

DECORATION

Bath, Michael
*Renaissance Decorative Painting in
Scotland*
N.M.S., 2003
ISBN: 1901663604

Prizeman, John
Your House, The Outside View
Quiller, 1982
ISBN: 0907621139

PLACES TO VISIT

MUSEUMS

GREAT BRITAIN

Avoncroft Museum of Historic
Buildings
Stokeheath
Bromsgrove
Worcestershire
B60 4JR
Tel: +44 (0)1527 831 363
www.avoncroft.org.uk

Hall i' th' Wood Museum
Green Way off Crompton Way
Bolton
Greater Manchester
BL1 8UA
Tel: +44 (0)1204 332370
www.boltonmuseums.org.uk

Museum of Welsh Life
St Fagans
Cardiff
CF5 6XB
Wales
Tel: +44 (0)29 2057 3500
www.ukattraction.com/south-wales

Ryedale Folk Museum
Hutton-le -Hole
Yorkshire
YO62 6VA
Tel: +44 (0)1751 417 367
www.ryedalefolkmuseum.co.uk

Weald & Downland Open Air
Museum
Singleton
Chichester
West Sussex
PO18 0EU
Tel: +44 (0)1243 811 363
www.wealddown.co.uk

ISLE OF MAN

Cregneash Folk Museum
Cregneash
IM9 5PT
Isle of Man
Tel: +44 (0)1624 648000
www.theheritagetrail.co.uk

NORTHERN IRELAND

Ulster Folk and Transport Museum
Cultra, Hollywood
BT 18 0EU
Co. Down
Tel: +44 (0)2890 428428
www.uftm.org.uk

HOUSES OPEN TO THE PUBLIC

GREAT BRITAIN

Craigievar Castle
Alford, Aberdeenshire
AB33 8JF
Scotland
Tel: +44 (0)1339 883 635
www.aboutbritain.com/craigievarcastle.htm
N.B. *The castle is closed for
renovation until Easter 2007*

Culross Palace
West Green House
Culross, Fife
KY12 8JH
Scotland
Tel: +44 (0)1383 880359
www.ukattraction.com/central-scotland/
culross-palace.htm

Gladstone's Land
477b Lawnmarket
Edinburgh
EH1 2NT
Scotland
Tel: +44 (0)131 226 5856
www.aboutbritain.com/gladstonesland.htm

Hampton Court Palace
East Molesey
Surrey
KT8 9AU
Tel: +44 (0)870 752 7777
www.historicroyalpalaces.org

Mary Queen of Scots' House
Jedburgh
Roxburghshire
Scotland
Tel: +44 01835 863331
www.rampantscotland.com

Plas Mawr
Conwy
North Wales
Tel: +44 02920 500200
www.conwy.com/plasmawr.html

Rufford Old Hall
Nr Ormskirk
Lancashire
L40 1SG
Tel:+44 (0)1704 821254
www.nationaltrust.org.uk/traveltrade

REPUBLIC OF IRELAND

Rothe House
Kilkenny
Ireland
Tel: +44 (0)56 7722893
www.kilkennyarchaeologicalsociety.ie/
rothehouse.htm

In addition, many towns and
villages are worth a visit, in
particular the following in England:
Lavenham (Suffolk), Chester
(Cheshire), and York (Yorkshire).

ABOUT THE AUTHOR

Brian Long has worn many hats in his time, starting out as a coal miner, then training as a teacher of ceramics and graphics, followed by a long spell as a forest officer. He has restored three period houses and one garden, as well as a Gothic Revival castle.

In his spare time he was Secretary, Editor, and then Chairman of the Association of Northumberland Local History Societies. A book on the castles of Northumberland and many papers on villages and period houses were to follow.

As a consequence of his work recording architectural details Brian was given the title 'Hon. Recorder' by the Association of Local History Societies. He is also a Fellow of the Regional Furniture Society and the Society of Antiquities for Scotland.

He is still recording building details and researching period furniture for future publications. He also attends specialist miniature fairs, where he retails his own authentic yet unusual miniatures and freely dispenses information to other enthusiasts.

Brian is always pleased to answer queries, and can be e-mailed at the following address:

brian@brianlong.wanadoo.co.uk

GLOSSARY

AUMBRY

Started out as a cupboard to hold 'alms', but became a cupboard of a more general nature.

BALDACCHINO

A rich canopy.

BRACE

A diagonal strut serving to stiffen a joint between horizontal and vertical members of a timber frame.

CLOSE STUDS

The spaces between the studs (vertical timbers) are approximately the same width as the studs.

CORBELLING

A projection of stone, brick or wood protruding from a wall to support a beam or truss.

CRENEL

Indentation in battlements. See also 'Crenellations'.

CRENELLATIONS

These, together with merlons, are the two parts of battlements. Merlons are the toothlike portion standing up between the opening, embrasure, or crenel. Together they become crenellations.

CRUCKS (CRUCK FRAME)

Matched curved timbers, made from one large log split down the centre, to form a matched pair.

DIAPER WORK

Diamond patterns in brickwork, made by using the ends of darker bricks (stone or tile could also be used).

FIELDED PANELS

Renaissance panels which have the greater part of their flat surface projecting beyond the face of the framing.

GNOMON

The part of the sundial that casts the shadow. Most were metal, but a few were stone, as in the carved faces on Scottish examples.

MERLONS

See 'Crenellations'.

MULLIONS

Vertical bars of stone or wood dividing a window opening into 'lights'.

NOGGING

Bricks used for filling gaps in a timber frame.

PARGETING

This now refers to external decorative plaster work, but in the sixteenth century it was also used for internal plaster decoration.

POTENCE

A wooden frame which carries a ladder in a dovecote.

PURLINS

A transverse horizontal beam in a roof carrying the common rafters.

QUATREFOILS

Four-leaved (literally): a circular or square opening that has tracery with four foils, leaflets, or petals.

QUOIN

A stone or brick used to reinforce an external corner or edge of a wall.

ROOD

Gallery across a room carried on a rood beam.

SPIT JACK

Mechanical device to turn a spit.

STUDS/STUDDING

Subsidiary members, usually vertical, in a timber-framed wall.

TRANSOMS

Horizontal bar across a mullioned window (*see* also 'Mullions').

TRUSS

A structure composed of a combination of members, usually in a triangular arrangement so as to form a rigid framework.

WATTLE AND DAUB

A wattle panel or frame inserted into a timber wall and then plastered over.

INDEX

GMC PUBLICATIONS

Castle Place, 166 High Street, Lewes, East Sussex BN7 1XU , United Kingdom

Tel: 01273 488005　Fax: 01273 402866　E-mail: pubs@thegmcgroup.com　Website: www.gmcbooks.com

Contact us for a complete catalogue, or visit our website. Orders by credit card are accepted.